IN PRAISE OF PRAYING FOR YOUR ADDICT

"What follows in these pages resonates with me, both organizationally and personally. For in these pages is something which originates neither in the cloister nor the laboratory, but rather in the crucible of human experience. While what comes out of either can inform and inspire, too often it may be detached from life in the world. In Praying for Your Addicted Loved One: 90 in 90*, author Sharron Cosby writes from personal experience, with all of its 'blood, sweat, toil, and tears."*

~Commissioner William A. Roberts, National Commander of The Salvation Army (excerpt from Foreword to *Praying for Your Addicted Loved One: 90 in 90*).

"Transparent, hopeful, and honest, Sharron Cosby writes with the quiet eloquence of a tried and tested warrior in the battlefield of addiction and compulsive behaviors. So often the process of recovery is placed solely on the shoulders of the addict. This devotional invites all the stakeholders to share in the suffering. As a clinician and counselor who has worked with addicts and their loved ones, I recommend Praying For Your Addicted Loved One *as a must-have companion for all family members who find themselves in the desert of addiction."*

~Peter J. Dell LCSW, Board Certified Diplomate in Clinical Social Work.

"I love this book! Praying for Your Addicted Loved One: 90 in 90 *is truly a God-send, not only for those living day-to-day with loved ones chained to addictions, but for those, like me, who need guidance in understanding the needs of neighbors and relatives struggling with relentless addictions. Sharron Cosby's insights and personal experiences lend heart and credibility to each brief, reader-friendly devotional, and she squeezes much meaning, hope, and application from each scripture."*

~Debora M. Coty, award-winning author of 13 inspirational books, including *Too Blessed to be Stressed* and *More Beauty, Less Beast, Fear, Faith and a Fistful of Chocolate.*

"DO NOT read another book, article, or advice column on coping with the addiction of someone you love until you have read this! Author Sharron Cosby gets it. After much pain, heartache, and frustration, she gets it. And you can too. As one who has also suffered through addiction issues in my life and with my own family, I can tell you that Praying for Your Addicted Loved One: 90 in 90 *will change your perspective about this issue once and for all."*

~Dr. Michael Hailey, Pastor, New Day Church, Brandon, FL.

"Sharron Cosby has the loving heart of a true Southern belle, and she opens that heart willingly, sharing her personal experiences as the parent of an addict. Drawing from the book of Jeremiah, Sharron's devotional uses scripture to provide hope and sound guidance in what can seem like a hopeless situation."

~Kat Heckenback, author of *Finding Angel, Seeking Unseen,* and multiple contributions to *Chicken Soup for the Soul,* anthologies, magazines, e-zines and artist.

"Praying for Your Addicted Loved One: 90 in 90 *is an education in divesting the bondage of addictive behaviors and substance abuse. The 90 devotions with soul-searching reflections, questions, and prayers, help us understand the reality and heartaches of both the addicted and those who love them."*

~Ruth Carmichael Ellinger, award-winning author of five books including *The Wildrose Trilogy* and *Women of the Secret Place*.

"The journey from a mother's despair to the kept promises of God comes through in each devotion. Readers will relate to Sharron's sojourn even if they are on a different path. They will find hope, encouragement, and inspiration no matter their circumstances."

~Lt. Colonel Martha Jewett, Divisional Director of Women's Ministries, The Salvation Army Florida Division.

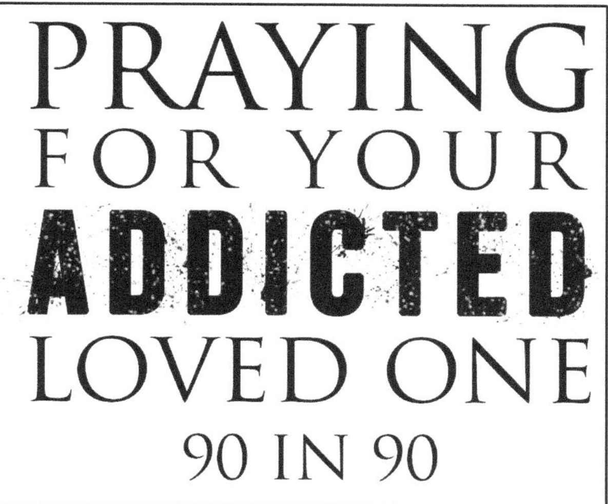

Sharron K. Cosby

Praying for Your Addicted Loved One: 90 in 90

First Print Edition: June 2013

ISBN 13: 978-1-62480-071-9
ISBN 10: 1-62480-071-8

Published by BookJolt, LLC, PO Box 1619, Auburn, WA 98071.

TABLE OF CONTENTS

DEDICATION

To my three children whose lives embody God's grace and redemption.
To troubled families—may you grab hold of God's
promises for your loved ones—and not let go.

ACKNOWLEDGMENTS

Burdens carried with a friend grow lighter and more tolerable, and I want to say *thank you* to those who lightened my load through the years.

I have three friends from work who listened to my tales of woe for days on end, held me as I sobbed, and prayed many prayers as I struggled with the chaos of my son's addiction. Debbie, Carolyn, and Paula, you hold a special place in my heart. You loved me through some of the worst years of my life.

I owe many thanks to my fellow critique buddies in Word Weavers of Tampa. You cleaned up my words and helped build my confidence as a writer. I knew my words were hitting their mark when you cried reading the stories aloud. Jan Powell, Kat Heckenbach, Kim Moore, and Kathryn Howard, thank you so much for cheering me on when I sometimes wanted to quit.

I also want to thank my editor, Adele Brinkley, for believing in the power of the story and for further polishing my words.

My precious ones, Caron, Josh, and Katie, without whom there is no story, thank you for allowing me to share our pain as an offering of hope, encouragement, and strength to other families experiencing similar struggles. I am proud of your accomplishments and am thankful God chose me to be your mother and now your friend. I love you more than words can express and each of you is my true favorite.

Without the constant love and support of my husband, Danny, I don't think I could have fared as well as I did. He was, and is, my safe place to run when the storms of life came my way. Our life isn't exactly the way I imagined it would be, but it has been an unforgettable journey of love and grace.

My grandchildren, Kody, Caleb, Mason, Cayden, and Caitlyn are the absolute joys of my life. When the drama of our lives reached its worst you were thankfully too young to recognize it. My prayer is that your life choices will steer you far away from the hurt and pain our family lived through.

To my mother, Tish Mills Knight, I owe my love of stringing words together. You instilled in me an insatiable hunger for books. But more importantly, you taught me to love in the toughest of circumstances and to trust God in all things. Thank you for believing in me.

To the hurting mothers I've met and wept with, thank you for sharing your hearts and hurts with me.

For those who consoled me through dark days, I'm forever grateful. All I can say is *thank you* to all who stood by our family. You share in our joy of lives restored and redeemed.

And to the prophet Jeremiah, I owe my life and sanity. I want to hug your neck one day when I'm in heaven. Until I read the words God laid on your heart in Jeremiah 30 and 31, I was a helpless, hopeless mess. Your clarion call to "restrain your voice from weeping and your eyes from tears" woke me up to the peace that passes understanding I had heard about all my life.

I am grateful my sweet Misi posted on Facebook: "Restoration Promised. Jeremiah 30 and 31."

> *"They will return from the land of the enemy. So there is hope for your future."*
>
> **Jeremiah 31:16b-17a NIV**

FOREWORD

From its very earliest days, The Salvation Army has addressed itself to addictions work and the effects of enslaving substances. One of the tenets of founder William Booth's effort to reach the poor and oppressed of his day was the "effectual deliverance of the drunkard." Our work in that area always has been to treat the victim in a respectful and redemptive manner, with a strong reliance on the Almighty. The problem is no less severe today, when estimates suggest as high as ten percent of the American population suffers from drug and alcohol abuse.

What follows in these pages resonates with me, both organizationally and personally. For in these pages is something which originates neither in the cloister nor the laboratory, but rather in the crucible of human experience. While what comes out of either of those places can inform and inspire, too often it may be detached from life in the world.

That is not the case here.

In *Praying For Your Addicted Loved One: 90 in 90*, author Sharron K. Cosby writes from personal experience, with all of its "blood, sweat, toil, and tears."

She allows us to see into her innermost being, sharing thoughts, feelings, and experiences that we feel privileged to know. In fact, we feel honored that she would entrust to us, the reader, that which is deep down in her soul.

There is no attempt here to sensationalize or to pander or to arouse unhealthy curiosity; rather, one finds here only a desire to be helpful for those who are traveling a similar road.

The Psalmist poses the question: "If the foundations are destroyed, what can the righteous do?" (Psalm 11:3 NASB). Sharron carefully and prayerfully guides and counsels using the words of the Old Testament prophet Jeremiah those whose foundations have been seemingly destroyed by a loved one enslaved by addiction. Often called the "weeping prophet," his words are especially helpful to those who find themselves shedding their own tears, both visible and those in places where no one can see—the tears shed in private.

The words of this weeping one are indeed helpful. God promised restoration, presence, inner satisfaction, indeed recovery, to those to whom they were first spoken, those who looked to him for aid and deliverance. Even a casual reading of Jeremiah's words suggests the help and hope one can receive still today.

Practitioners and professionals have practiced and applied their techniques, theories, and therapies, which all have their place and are proven helpful. But, in the end, it is by the grace of God that one recovers and stays recovered, that families and friends can find comfort and support.

By sharing so openly, a story of divine grace will be shared with each reader. May it please God to be so.

Commissioner William A. Roberts
National Commander
The Salvation Army

INTRODUCTION

I couldn't sleep. Visions of Josh, my 33-year-old son, arrested or dead, competed with the Sandman. My nerves were as frayed as old towels in the hall closet. Would I ever find peace and rest? I dragged myself out of bed and went into the living room prepared to watch television, but reached for my Bible instead.

Months prior to this night, my daughter-in-law, Misi, posted on Facebook: "Restoration Promised. Jeremiah 30 and 31." When I saw her entry, I didn't read the verses. The possibility of restoration hadn't entered my mind, so why bother? I remembered the references as I sat on the couch clutching my Bible. I flipped to chapter 30. "Restoration is Promised" declared the chapter heading.

I wept.

In 2008, after three clean and sober years, Josh relapsed again—hard. Prior to the crash on pain pills, he managed to right himself when he slipped, but this time he faced a powerful and unforgiving enemy: opiate painkillers. The chokehold on Josh and our family grew tighter every day.

Josh's addiction reached an all-time high in 2009. His behavior transitioned from borrowing money from me to stealing. Pilfered cash shattered trust in my son. Tools and jewelry vanished. Family relationships crumbled.

Sitting on my couch on October 8, 2009 my life changed. The Lord promised restoration to his children and to bring them home. He promised to break the bonds that held them captive. I needed to hear and believe this was possible for my family. Hope burrowed deep into my heart.

I marked my Bible, inserting Josh's name in place of Israel, Jacob, and Ephraim. I read and reread those chapters and prayed them aloud. I cried out to God for restoration of my son and family. I wrote at Jeremiah 30:8: "I will break the yoke off Josh's neck and will tear off the bonds of drugs, alcohol, lying and friends; no longer will drugs enslave him." I made the verse mine.

The readings in *Praying for Your Addicted Loved One: 90 in 90* focus on Jeremiah 30 and 31. Jeremiah prophesied to Israel over a forty-year period during the reign of five kings. His message provoked anger but also provided the stimulus for the Israelites to repent and return to God. Some of the readings may ignite anger in you—anger at yourself for allowing certain behaviors within your family. Or anger at your addicted loved one for the situation your family is in, or a mixture of both. Hang on to the end, allowing God's salve of restoration and redemption to quiet your soul.

The daily readings reflect the Twelve-Step philosophy for newly recovering addicts. If you are unfamiliar with this way of life, one of the first instructions is to attend ninety meetings (Narcotics Anonymous, Alcoholics Anonymous, Sexual Addictions Anonymous, Celebrate Recovery, etc.) in ninety days. The ninety days provides sufficient time to establish different, positive habits, and to learn to invest in new people, places, and things. At the same time, you, as a family member, support your addict with a daily Bible reading and prayer.

I use the term *addict* to describe all forms of life-controlling behaviors and substances: alcoholism, drugs, gambling, sex addict, anorexia, etc.

Praying for Your Addicted Love One: 90 in 90 was written for families plowing through the sludge of addiction—without hope, peace, and encouragement. Experience God's touch as you study the scripture verses, read glimpses of our family's story, and record your responses to the quiet time prompts.

I never imagined my family would travel the road called addiction. The potholes were deep, the highways bumpy, and tragedies occurred along the way. But God's grace carried us through each bump and hole, one day at a time.

I invite you to join with me as we pray for our addicted loved ones.

DAY 1: GOD'S STORY AND MINE

This is the word that came to Jeremiah from the Lord, "Write in a book all the words I have spoken to you. The days are coming when I will bring my people Israel and Judah back from captivity and restore them to the land I gave their forefathers to possess."

Jeremiah 30:2-3 NIV

I love books. Always have. Always will. My mother passed on her love of reading and it stuck like multi-colored sprinkles on an ice cream cone. There's nothing sweeter in my world than a good book and a cup of steaming hot coffee.

God knew that one day the events of our family's journey would be told as a means of helping others in similar situations. Three attempts at writing our story fell short. I found no satisfaction in rehashing all the bad things our family experienced over the years. The story made me sad, so I shelved the idea. But God had plans for those experiences.

The Cosby saga is another tale among thousands. You and I probably aren't that much different from one another. We go to work, raise our children, cook dinner at night, worship each week, pay our taxes, and have an addict in our family.

On October 8, 2009, when I collapsed into the lap of Jeremiah 30 and 31, I decided to write a book about God's story—not my story.

I chose to write about what changed my life that early October morning instead of retelling the negatives of my family. The book is about the One who spoke life, health, and encouragement into my worn-out heart. The real story is the scriptures in Jeremiah 30 and 31 that caught my attention like a drill sergeant barking orders. But the Holy Spirit's touch was gentle. He didn't shake me up and smack me around. He quietly and gently wrapped me in his arms and whispered, "Go ahead, Sharron, cry your tears of sorrow; tomorrow I will bring you tears of joy."

Do you write words of hope and encouragement to your addict? You don't have to write a book or a short story. A simple heartfelt note from you is a tangible reminder of your love apart from the drugs or alcohol. Start small. Test the waters with "I love you and I've missed spending time with you." These words can open doors to a renewed relationship.

DAILY PRAYER

Father, bless my words as I speak and write to my loved one. May my words be acceptable in your sight and soothing to his spirit. Grant that I choose my words wisely, to build up and not tear down, to encourage and speak words of life. Amen.

REFLECTION

Consider journaling what God is doing in your life. Jot down thoughts about your loved one.

DAY 2: DEALING WITH THE PAIN

Oh, my anguish, my anguish! I writhe in pain. Oh, the agony of my heart! My heart pounds within me, I cannot keep silent ... Disaster follows disaster; the whole land lies in ruins. In an instant my tents are destroyed.

Jeremiah 4:19a NIV

As parents, we grieve when our children misbehave. Spouses experience disillusionment when their partner acts inappropriately. How do we handle bad behavior, whether by a child, a spouse or a parent?

During their teenage years, our three children acted out contrary to their upbringing. My husband and I were ill prepared for most of the situations in which we found ourselves. I often didn't handle myself well. I was distraught. I cried. I yelled. I blamed God. After all, I had been a good girl and couldn't understand why all this bad stuff was happening to me.

The scripture for today encapsulates my emotions during those fifteen years. On November 8, 2009, I wrote in the margin beside the verse, "That's how I feel. I hold my pain inside. It never seems to end. One thing after another seems to strike our family. I'm so tired."

The stress of having an addict in the family manifested itself in migraine headaches, stomach upsets, and depression. I tried to handle the problems on my own, but they became too much for me.

It was through reading Jeremiah 30 and 31, fifteen years later, that I finally relinquished my son to God's care.

What about you? Is your heart in agony over a child? A spouse? A grandchild? Are you physically exhausted because of worrying over what could happen? Join me on this journey to restoration and redemption. Allow the peace that passes all understanding to wash over you, bringing rest and comfort.

DAILY PRAYER

Dear Father, I bring my anguished heart to you today. I lay it at your feet and in faith I believe you will hold me in the palm of your hand, to comfort me as only you can. Your Word says that the Lord is close to the brokenhearted and saves those who are crushed in spirit. Draw close tonight. Amen.

REFLECTION

Describe your most recent moments of anguish with your addict. How did you manage your feelings or the situation?

DAY 3: RELEASE YOUR FEARS

Cries of fear are heard—terror, not peace.

Jeremiah 30:5 NIV

I have lived most of my life in fear. Fear of failure. Fear of poverty. Fear of sickness and death. Fear for my children's safety. Terror and fear knocked at our home's door more than once over the course of the past fifteen years.

I handle fear by bottling it up. I hold it close like a security blanket. It's tattered and worn, but it's comfortable—something I know well. My anxiousness never changed the circumstances; it only made me sick. I learned that fear will eat me alive if left unchecked. Most of what I feared never came to pass.

Life with an addict naturally breeds fear. I know what it's like to lie in bed waiting to hear the garage door go up signaling a teen's safe return home. I know the panic of a late-night phone call, wondering if it's a sheriff telling me my child is dead or arrested. I understand the uncertainty of a drug overdose—will he live, die, or be disabled in some way?

I have never been afraid *of* my children, only afraid *for* them. They put themselves in situations with potentially disastrous outcomes. The fear of what could happen was more than I could wrestle with at times.

As I began to read scriptures on rest and peace, I realized that even in the midst of what was happening in my home, a peaceful spirit was still mine for the taking. I could not control the circumstances, but I could control my responses and maintain a level head. I learned to tap into that quiet spirit through daily scripture reading and prayer.

The road to recovery is a day-by-day process of trusting in the One who offers rest and comfort in the face of fear and terror. Trusting our addict is also a day-by-day progression as we lay aside the past and look forward to a different future free from anguish and dread.

Does fear drive the engine of your home? Begin to name your fears and develop some action plans to combat them. You may find that much of what causes an increased heart rate never occurs. It is one thing to tremble at something concrete, such as an arrest or an overdose; it is another to wreck your health over imaginations.

As you begin this ninety-day journey, take baby steps toward releasing your fears into God's capable hands. You will be amazed at the amount of peace that will envelop your life.

Fear is not God's best for us. He desires that we live in peace.

DAILY PRAYER

Precious Lord, I pray for peace in my family tonight. Surround us with your peace, the kind that passes all understanding, the kind the world cannot give. I surrender my fears to you, asking that you go before me, that you gather my family under your wings and provide refuge for the days ahead. Amen.

REFLECTION

Describe how dread and terror have invaded your home. How do you handle fear?

(1) Fear of someone breaking in our home & Barry being too drunk to do anything

(2) Constant fear of saying the wrong thing & starting [illegible]

(3) Constant fear of making any noise while he slept (passed out of course) in fear of him waking up & calling me every name in the book.

(4) Constant fear of him ever driving knowing that his blood alcohol level was off the charts.

(5) Constant fear of committing to anything not wanting to be embarrassed or humiliated in front of family & friends.

DAY 4:
THAT HARD FIRST STEP

Then why do I see every strong man with his hands on his stomach like a woman in labor, every face turned deathly pale? How awful that day will be! None will be like it. It will be a time of trouble for Jacob, but he will be saved out of it.

Jeremiah 30:6b–7 NIV

My pastor challenged our congregation to observe a Daniel Fast as part of our New Year's celebration. The fast is based on the actions of Daniel in the Old Testament when the Israelites were taken into captivity by the Babylonians. The fast lasted twenty-one days during which we ate only fruits, vegetables, and grains and drank nothing but water.

Being a regular dieter, I thought the fast would be a piece of cake; however, my body had other ideas. I missed two days of work because of muscle cramps in my feet and legs. I writhed on the bed in excruciating pain. The response to caffeine deprivation was horrific. As I tossed and turned I thought, "This must be what it's like to go through drug withdrawal." I seriously considered drinking a pot of coffee at 2 a.m. to ease the vise-like pain in my legs. I pressed through the agony without caving in to the caffeine temptation.

That experience provided me with a small peek into an addict's life. It is easy to say, "Just be strong. Only a weak person gives in. You must not really want to be clean, otherwise, you wouldn't keep using."

Our verses for today paint a picture of men in childbirth, but they could as easily describe the agonies of withdrawal. It is an awful experience to go through, both as participant and observer. The body is demanding its regular supply of the addictive substance and the deficiency results in agonizing discomfort.

After a period of using drugs or drinking alcohol, the lure of the substance is to keep the pain away and not for the fleeting pleasure. The user no longer consumes for the taste or the euphoria, he or she just doesn't want to hurt. Pain fuels the abuse.

Only once did I see my son withdraw from pain pills. It broke my heart to know that his suffering was self-induced and that it was avoidable.

It's easier to stay clean than to get clean. The first step is the hardest.

DAILY PRAYER

Dear Father, bless those who struggle through withdrawal. Be ever present through the temptation to use substances again to ease the pain. May your Holy Spirit substitute peace for pain—both for the user and for the family who loves him. Amen.

REFLECTION

Has your addicted loved one gone through physical withdrawals? Write down some of the emotions you experienced during that time.

Barry was sedated through most all of his withdrawal period; it was devastating watching him go thru withdrawals; he was very combative so they had to tie arms & legs down; when he did wake up he was so confused; I went thru so many different emotions during his time in ICU feelings I never knew even existed; it was one of the most difficult times I have ever gone thru.

DAY 5: HELD HOSTAGE

In that day, declares the LORD Almighty, I will break the yoke off their necks and will tear off their bonds; no longer will foreigners enslave them.

Jeremiah 30:8 NIV

When I first read this portion of scripture, I wrote in the margin of my Bible the things that held my son captive: drugs, alcohol, lying, friends. I put the date when I read the verses and began praying specifically that God would release the bands of steel keeping him bound.

Can you name what binds your addicted loved one? Is it pornography? Gambling? Sex? Friends? There are a host of substances and behaviors that exert control. Put a name on the enemy and stand firm against it based on God's Word. I encourage you to write in your Bible the exact substance or behavior causing trouble and begin to pray for its removal.

Each time I read the scriptures, I reread my handwritten bondage words so that my heart would be reminded of them and be encouraged. Not every day closed in victory, but the seeds of faith were planted and then watered with my tears. Each time I prayed, I reminded God of his promise to restore my home and my son.

Personalize these scriptures so you will understand how much God cares for your loved ones. He knows every hair on their heads and every stone that causes them to stumble. Our heavenly Father wants to make them whole more than you want them restored.

Family members are held hostage along with their addict. The emotional, relational, and financial tolls leads many families to the breaking point. Feelings of shame and guilt are relentless taskmasters, driving the wedge deeper until the rift is beyond repair. Professional counseling may be required to restore a sense of stability to the family unit. Don't be afraid to ask for help.

Breaking chains of bondage is hard work but the end result is liberating.

DAILY PRAYER

Lord of the liberated, hold my loved one's hand as the stranglehold of addictions drops like rocks, one heavy thud at a time. Fill the empty places with your sweet Holy Spirit. Guide each step closer to your throne of grace. Amen.

REFLECTION

What holds your loved one in bondage? What can you do to encourage him to shake loose from the choices that enslave him and your family? Is there something holding you by the scruff of the neck?

Alcohol

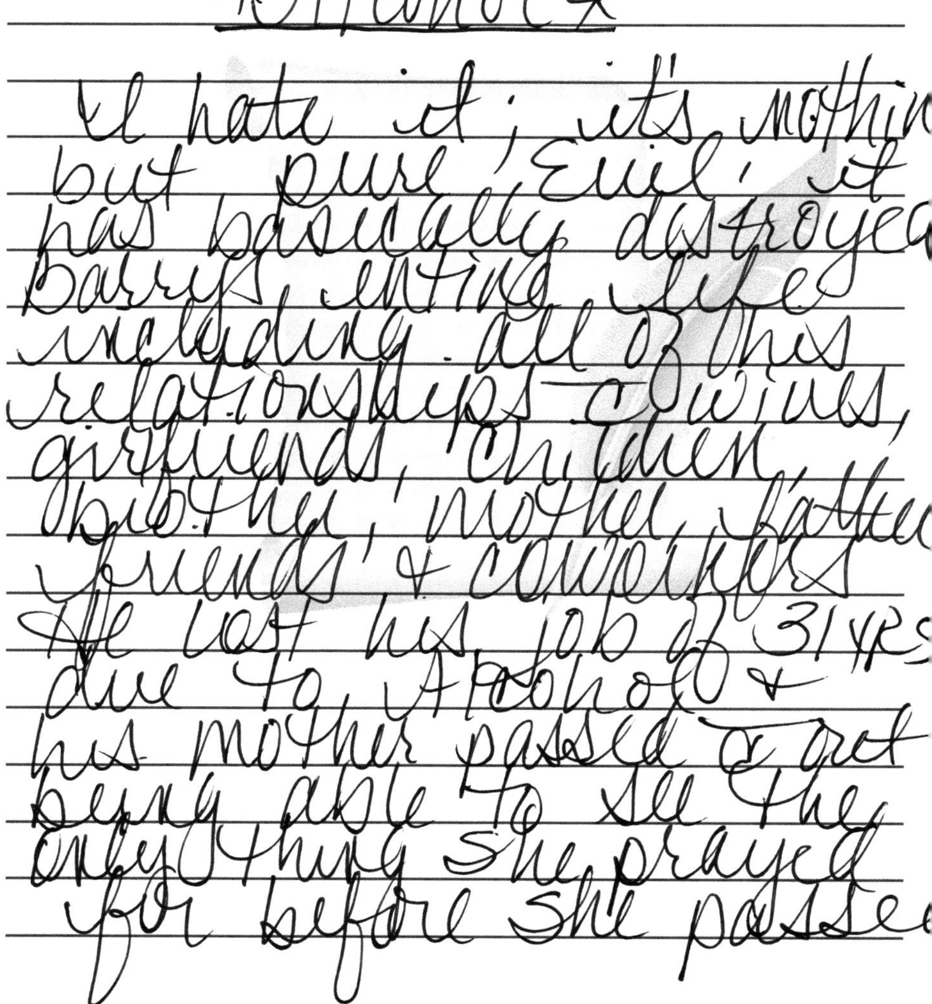

I hate it; it's nothing but pure Evil; it has basically destroyed Barry's entire life including all of his relationships w/ wives, girlfriends, children, brother, mother, father, friends & coworkers. He lost his job of 31 yrs due to Alcohol & his mother passed & not being able to see the only thing she prayed for before she passed

DAY 6: LOST IN THE WILDERNESS

I will surely save you out of a distant place, your descendants from the land of their exile. Jacob will again have peace and security, and no one will make him afraid.

Jeremiah 30:10:b NIV

Our family relocated from Alabama to Florida in 1992. At the time of the move, my father told me we were heading to a different environment and to be careful. I scoffed at his warning, but later realized he was right. People of many diverse cultures made our city their home and the result was various norms. We moved from the Bible Belt to an area that, though saturated with churches, held a different outlook on acceptable behaviors. Many of our children's friends were not involved in church. Our new home brought challenges for which we were unprepared.

Is that your experience? Is yours a mobile family, moving for job promotions, military assignments, or family responsibilities? Did the move adversely affect your children?

As parents, we make tough decisions that impact family members. These decisions are made with the best interests of everyone at the forefront of our reasoning. However, that doesn't mean there won't be fallout. It does mean we won't continually beat ourselves up for making a move to better our family's situation. We second-guessed our choice to relocate many times.

The distant land of addiction is a place no parent or spouse ever dreams of visiting, although many of us find our tents pitched in that desolate, lonely place. The landscape is bleak, empty, and bereft of happiness. Heartache and depression penetrate our spirits like giant trees putting down roots. But, today's verse offers encouragement. God's Word says that he will save our loved ones from that detached place—addiction—and we will again have peace and security and won't be afraid.

Moving from familiar surroundings creates stress for family members. Acknowledge the anxiety and have age-appropriate discussions with your family. Use these talking times to restore a sense of calm. The same holds for recovery. Helping your family understand the way out of addiction is not easy. It takes time and courage. It requires changing the familiar routine of activities and friends. Recovery is a new road map for living.

The journey may seem long, but at its end awaits rewards of great beauty.

DAILY PRAYER

Dear Father, thank you for the journey through the wilderness called addiction. Open my eyes to your promises. Open my arms to receive your grace and mercy, and help me extend them to my addict. Amen.

REFLECTION

Has your family changed locations? Did you feel like you were in a foreign land? How did you help your children adjust to the move?

DAY 7: REDIRECTING BEHAVIOR

... I will discipline you but only in due measure; I will not let you go entirely unpunished.

Jeremiah 30:11b NIV

The main difference in discipline and punishment is the motivation. Discipline has at its core a redirection of behavior. Punishment carries with it a punitive motive. Both are necessary when dealing with addicts.

Parents or spouses of addicts walk a fine line between the two extremes. We correct our children in an effort to redirect their behavior, but sometimes we are harsh and vengeful and cross over into punishment. I think the latter comes from frustration and helplessness. We've tried being nice and understanding only to have our loved ones continue in their bad behaviors. We've sent them to treatment centers (discipline) only to have them come out and continue in their addictions, leaving us, the family, bearing the financial responsibilities and emotional wreckage.

God loved the children of Israel more than anything. They were the apple of his eye, the chosen people. Because of their disobedience, he chastised them and they suffered the consequences.

We should hold our addicts responsible. Parents and spouses often overlook their addict's poor decisions until the final straw is tossed and their world collapses. Sometimes it's easier to let the deeds go uncorrected, but that approach is unfair to our addicts. It teaches them to sidestep responsibility and consequences. At some point, the legal system may step in and impose punishment rather than discipline and our options are wrenched from us. Act now while alternative solutions remain available.

Helping our children learn early on that consequences are tied to behaviors will go a long way in preparing them for life in the real world.

DAILY PRAYER

Father, guide me in redirecting my loved one. I can discipline fairly because your Word teaches that the Lord disciplines those he loves, as a father does the son he delights in. Fill my heart with a renewed love and hope for my addict. Amen.

REFLECTION

What is the difference between discipline and punishment? Do you exercise one or both on your addicted loved one?

DAY 8: UNDERSTANDING DEPENDENCE

Your wound is incurable, your injury beyond healing.
Jeremiah 30:12b NIV

For as long as I can remember, my Grandmother Knight was an insulin-dependent diabetic. Much of her day revolved around the kitchen, making certain she ate the proper foods at the proper time. She adjusted her life to the disease. Diabetes is a chronic, incurable disease.

I loved my grandmother.

My son has a chronic disease called addiction. Much of his day revolves around staying clean and sober. He adjusts his life to the disease.

I love my son.

I follow the medical model, that is, addiction is a disease for which there is no cure. There is treatment, but no cure apart from divine intervention. In clinical terms the word *abuse* has been replaced by the word *dependence.* Addiction has been extended to include mood-altering behaviors or activities such as gambling and pornography—even playing video games or smartphone usage.

Understanding that Josh's long-term drug and alcohol usage affected his brain helped me cope with the disease of addiction. It eased my anxiety to realize his poor choices came from an altered brain, not because he purposefully chose to do wrong. His ability to choose wisely was compromised. That didn't negate his responsibility and accountability for his actions, but it helped explain the reasons for them.

What can you do to gain information about this disease called addiction? Resources abound that provide non-scientific explanations. I encourage you to avail yourself of them. Knowledge increases understanding.

Today's scripture paints a picture of hopelessness and futility, but God didn't forsake the children of Israel. He tells them the truth and then in the next few verses provides hope. Many times we feel the situation with our addict is hopeless, but as God provided a way for the children of Israel, he will do the same for us and our families. We can help our addicts understand the truth about addiction and walk with them through recovery. That doesn't mean we don't hold them responsible, just that we love them in spite of their disease.

Understanding goes a long way in extending grace.

DAILY PRAYER

Lord, I lay my addict at your feet. I trust you with all my heart and will not depend on my understanding of your ways. I am thankful you make my way straight as I acknowledge your presence in my life. Amen.

REFLECTION

Do you think addiction is a disease or a lack of willpower? Familiarize yourself with current addiction research to better understand your addict's behaviors.

DAY 9: THE POWER OF FRIENDS

You're a burned-out case, as good as dead. Everyone has given up on you. All your fair-weather friends have skipped town without giving you a second thought.

Jeremiah 30:13-14a MSG

Friends are important to young and old alike. Although we treasure and protect our friendships, sometimes they prove lethal.

My son went into his first treatment center at sixteen and stayed twenty-eight days. He maintained his sobriety for about two months. We received a phone call one Friday night saying, "They've taken Josh to the hospital." The friend didn't say if he was dead or alive. Neither did he say to which hospital the ambulance raced. My husband and I sped to our community hospital hoping to find him there.

When we arrived, a nurse rushed us to the emergency room where we found our son in a four-point restraint, his limbs secured to the bed. "Mom, I uv u," he said. I thought he had suffered a stroke. I wondered if he would ever speak normally again.

When Josh looked at his dad, he recoiled as far as the restraints allowed. Visions of Danny's beard oozing in and out of his skin continued as the LSD-induced hallucinations assaulted his mind. His blood pressure spiked and plummeted. We endured a long night, waiting for the LSD, marijuana, and alcohol to leave his body.

Josh later recounted prior to leaving our home that Friday afternoon he ingested two hits of LSD on blotter paper, a gift from a "friend." He went to a young man's house for a night-long party while his parents were out of town. He took more LSD and drank copious amounts of alcohol and smoked marijuana. At some point, Josh experienced a grand mal seizure. Most of his friends ran, leaving him alone. One guy didn't run. Ironically he was on house arrest and shouldn't have been at the party in the first place. I thank God he was. He held Josh's tongue until the emergency personnel arrived, and then he left.

Josh admitted many years after this event that his friends didn't "have his back" like he thought they did. They deserted him in a time of great need.

Our children are often misguided thinking their friends will be with them forever.

Now that my son is in recovery, his friends have changed. He doesn't hang out with the kids from high school. He chooses people he meets in the Narcotics Anonymous rooms, those who share a common desire for sobriety. They are safe.

Be vigilant in praying for your children's companions; they might be hurting as much as your child.

Choosing friends is an important decision for young people and adults—choose wisely.

DAILY PRAYER

Lord, I thank you for the people in my addict's life. Your word says there is a friend that loves at all times, and a brother is born for adversity. Bring those kinds of folks into my loved one's path. Amen.

REFLECTION

Who are your addict's friends? Write down their names here. Have you ever prayed for them?

DAY 10: GETTING HEALTHY

But I will restore you to health and heal your wounds, declares the Lord.

Jeremiah 30:17

Our bodies are amazing. But, drugs, alcohol, and risky sexual behaviors take their toll. Some drugs eat away tooth enamel leaving decaying nubs. Alcohol destroys the stomach, liver, and brain cells. Our bodies weren't created to process chemicals and they literally wear out. Sexually transmitted diseases wreak havoc, leaving life-long consequences. Sometimes the damage is beyond repair.

In 2005 my son experienced a period of sobriety. He had a job. Life was good. He required extensive dental work, but because of his drug abuse history, the dentist didn't prescribe painkillers. Instead he wrote a prescription for an anti-inflammatory medicine. The pain from the dental work was severe, so Josh took more than the prescribed dosage plus over-the-counter ibuprofen. His stomach lining was weak from alcohol and drug abuse and the medicine caused a medical emergency.

He began passing and vomiting blood. My husband decided to take him to the hospital, but Josh collapsed at the front door before they could leave the house. Danny called 911. Josh was taken by ambulance to the emergency room where blood transfusions began. In all, he received nine units of blood. His body holds eleven. Several days in the hospital allowed him to begin healing.

Over time the body often repairs much of the damage caused

by substance abuse and alcohol consumption. Restoration of an addict's body requires not only abstinence from drugs and alcohol but lifestyle changes as well. A regimen of daily exercise and healthy nutrition is vital to reestablishing health.

The body is not the only broken part of your addict; his or her spirit is also broken. Lying, stealing, manipulating family and friends, and abusing drugs or alcohol takes an emotional toll. Family activities are a step toward restoring rifts in relationships.

Work together as a family at improving health and choosing activities that promote a better lifestyle. Preparing nutritious meals together is a way to eat better and restore relationships. Recreational activities like bowling, putt-putt golf, and other community resources are safe environments in which to repair strained family connections.

God wants your family healed and renewed—body, mind, and spirit.

DAILY PRAYER

Father, I thank you that you are close to the brokenhearted and that you save those who are crushed in spirit. Be especially near to my loved one tonight, healing his body, his soul, and his spirit. Help me initiate the healing. Amen.

REFLECTION

How is your addicted loved one's health? Are regular exercise and nutrition priorities? Does your family participate in physical activities together?

DAY 11: REACHING THE END

... because they all gave up on you and dismissed you as hopeless, that good-for-nothing Zion.

Jeremiah 30:17b MSG

Where is the truth in the saying, "Sticks and stones may break my bones, but words will never hurt me"? Words do cut and wound. Sometimes the scars of bitter, hateful words cut deeper than a knife. Hurtful comments haunt our memories, sinking deep roots into our very souls.

It would be easier some days to pack up our loved ones' belongings, put them at the curb, and forget they were ever born. Time and time again, they have betrayed our trust, stolen from us, and done all kinds of wicked things against our families. However, they are people we love. Often they are the children we birthed and nurtured, and it's almost impossible to walk away.

Perhaps you have family members and friends who encourage you to turn your back on your son, daughter, or spouse.

"Forget about him."

"He's a no-good drunk."

"She's nothing but a junkie."

The rest of the family has written them off. Sometimes turning your back seems the best solution to an out-of-control situation. But, your loved one is still there, still hurting.

Circumstances do arise when putting a loved one out of your home is necessary. We put our son out of our home after a week-long-cocaine-and-Xanax binge. We had done all we could to help him, but nothing worked. He checked into a homeless shelter and stayed there several months. He graduated from the shelter's addiction treatment program on my birthday in 2001.

We put him out of our home, but not out of our hearts. He was loved more during that time than any other up to that point. He was broken and hurting, but we couldn't fix him. During that time we remained hopeful God would work a miracle in his life. He was still breathing, and with each breath, hope remained alive.

When your addict reaches the end of himself or herself, it may be the knowledge of your love that helps him or her make the right choices that will lead to wholeness and sobriety.

Hopeless shifts to hopeful when love and caring are extended to the down and out.

DAILY PRAYER

Dear Lord, guide my actions and my words toward my loved one. I know that faith is being sure of what I hope for and certain of what I cannot see. With all my heart, I believe you are extending hope to my hopeless one. Amen.

REFLECTION

Have you given up on your addict? Have family members and friends walked away in disgust?

DAY 12: THE REWARDS OF COMPASSION

I'll turn things around for Jacob. I'll compassionately come in and rebuild homes.

Jeremiah 30:18a MSG

"There's no way I'll ever let you back in this house! You've hurt me for the last time. I will never trust you again."

Sound familiar? We've probably all said a similar thing to our addict. The pain of past hurts looms large when confronted with the possibility of heaping another blow on already battered emotions. But we do it. We put our hearts in line for disappointments time and time again. Why? Because we love our addicts in spite of their behaviors.

The verse for today declares God's promise to the children of Israel. He reminds them that with compassion he will rebuild not only the physical city of Jerusalem, but also their lives. That's what God longed for, to have Israel's heart. He desired their complete devotion. He wanted them to sell out for him, to worship no other gods.

As parents or spouses of an addict, we long for that kind of devotion from our loved one. We want to be valued more than drugs, alcohol, or addictive behaviors. It is a long, hard road to reach that level of commitment, but with God's help, our addicts can do it. We can, as well, as we stand beside them. We can give them precedence over busy work schedules, time tapping away at a home computer, and talking on a cell phone.

One problem we confront is that we lack God's patience. We tire of broken promises, missed appointments, unobserved curfews—the list goes on and on. We give up and sometimes walk away in disgust. But, by arming ourselves with holy promises, we can do all things through Christ who gives us strength, even loving the addicts in our lives.

Compassion implies that we will step into their shoes and walk through the dark days with them. Is this an easy task to fulfill? Of course not. Our loved ones have hurt us over and over, most of the time unintentionally. The addiction drives the engine of their lives, leaving them in a derailed heap. Compassion reaches down deep, beyond the hole in our hearts, and loves again.

DAILY PRAYER

Jesus, as you looked out on Jerusalem and were moved with compassion for your children, touch my heart tonight as I step into the boat with my addict and love him through this time in his life. May my caring concern bring rewards in due time. Amen.

REFLECTION

What will it take for the situation to turn around in your home? Who will take the first step toward reconciliation?

DAY 13: HEALING LAUGHTER

Thanksgivings will pour out of the windows; laughter will spill through the doors. Things will get better and better. Depression days are over.

Jeremiah 30:19a MSG

It's difficult to joke around when your home is flooded with hurt. An old-fashioned belly laugh breaks the tension, providing much-needed relief. You know the kind—your face hurts from smiling like a mule eating briars. Your stomach muscles ache with out-of-the-ordinary usage. Tears stream from your eyes because you're laughing so long and hard. Laughter is a stress buster that God approves. In Proverbs 15:13 (NIV) we read, "A happy heart makes the face cheerful, but heartache crushes the spirit."

I think one of God's rewards for persisting with our addicts are those moments of levity and humor. He knows the weight in our soul and allows us to see the light side of an event so we can laugh instead of cry.

When my children were in their teens, honoring curfew was a foreign concept to them. One morning about 2 a.m., Josh and one of our daughters were not home as instructed. My husband was in Mexico on business. Our youngest daughter and I went in search for the two errant children. Katie suggested someone's home as a possible hunting ground, so off we went. We got out of the car and began tiptoeing between two houses. My shoes had little metal leaves on them that jingled with each step.

Katie began to giggle as I tried to sneak up on the friend's house. "*Shhh*, you'll wake the neighbors!" I could just imagine someone shooting at us or calling the sheriff. We still enjoy the humor of our early morning sleuthing. Oh, dear friend, I needed some comic relief in my life during that time.

What about you? Is your heart heavy from its non-stop burden of living with an addict? Has your face forgotten what a smile looks like? There's no time like the present to change, even if you're in the middle of a trying time with your loved one.

Look for moments when you can throw open the windows of your heart and laugh. Feel it from the top of your head to the soles of your feet. Let it work wonders like a medicine.

Times of laughter may be few, but they are greatly cherished.

DAILY PRAYER

Lord, thank you for the bright spots in my day. Thank you for making the rough places less bumpy with doses of humor. Thank you for memories of good times with my children. I will praise you every time I think of them. Amen.

REFLECTION

What can your family do to restore laughter to your home? Recall a pleasant time spent with your addicted loved one and consider discussing it with him or her.

DAY 14: STAND BY ME

Their leader will be one of their own; their ruler will arise from among them.

Jeremiah 30:21 NIV

Oftentimes, the parent is the addict and the family is thrown into a tailspin because it has no leader. There is no one to guide the other members to live according to God's direction. What happens in this situation? Who takes charge when Mom or Dad is incapable to lead the family because of his or her addiction?

There are many questions but often few answers. Our verse today says that a ruler will arise from among the family. That may mean an older sibling will step in and run the household. If the offending parent is the mother, then the father will have to perform some of the wife's duties and vice versa. God will provide a leader during this time, and he promises to draw that individual close to his heart.

If your family members are children, they will be unable to fulfill responsible positions. It may mean that an extended family member temporarily fills the role as leader of your home. Prayerfully ask God for wisdom to provide the right person in your home to serve as the physical and emotional protector.

God's desire is for our families to be whole and safe. When circumstances thwart God's best, he allows someone else to stand in the gap. New leadership can relieve the chaos and conflict arising from the addict's misbehavior. Ravaged emotions can heal.

This reprieve can bring periods of laughter and lightheartedness. Allow this leader time to establish your family on firm footing.

DAILY PRAYER

Father, draw near to my family today. Guide someone to intersect with our lives who will bring stability and peace to a house full of chaos. Bless me as I acknowledge you in all my ways even as you direct my paths. Amen.

REFLECTION

Who is the leader in your home? Is it the addict? How has his or her addiction impacted the family?

DAY 15: THROUGH THICK AND THIN

So you will be my people, and I will be your God.
Jeremiah 30:22 NIV

In the book of Ruth, Naomi and her daughters-in-law found themselves with no husbands, no land, and no future. Naomi released the young women from their commitment to her following their husbands' deaths, but Ruth loved Naomi and did not want to leave her. In a memorialized exchange, Ruth pledged herself to take care of Naomi by saying, "Where you go I will go, and where you stay I will stay. Your people will be my people and your God my God" (Ruth 1:16b NIV).

Ruth loved her mother-in-law so much she vowed she would share Naomi's kinsmen and her God.

Do we love our addict enough to vow to remain with him or her through thick or thin? That is a hard question to answer after a major fight erupts. Sometimes a nanosecond is all it would take for you to pack up and move out. Other times, a heartfelt discussion of available options is appropriate and the desire to stay entices your mind and heart.

The recovery community is full of brokenhearted people whose parents, siblings, spouses, children, and friends walked out on them when life got tough. What most of our wounded loved ones need is for someone to say, "Where you go, I will go. Your God will be my God." They need to know that someone is willing to stay and help them fight for their very lives. The camaraderie in many

Twelve-Step meeting rooms is palpable, and the participants know they are loved and have a common bond—recovery.

Most NA and AA meetings end with the participants holding hands in a circle repeating the Serenity Prayer. When they break apart, the bear hugs start. "I love ya, man," is a common greeting in the rooms. They have found their people, and they are working on finding their God.

God calls each of us to be one of his people. He longs to be our God and for us to follow his teachings and experience the life he has available for us.

Many times the challenge comes in letting him be God and getting to know his people.

DAILY PRAYER

Lord, thank you for the people my loved one now calls his own. Thank you for the support he receives from them and that together they will find their way to you. Amen.

REFLECTION

When the chips are down and there is trouble, on which family member or friend do you call for help? Do you call God's name only in desperation?

DAY 16: DREAMING AND HOPING

The fierce anger of the LORD will not turn back until he fully accomplishes the purposes of his heart. In days to come you will understand this.

Jeremiah 30:24 NIV

As each of my children was born, I dreamed of what they would be when grown. I wanted one to be a doctor, one a dentist, and one a lawyer. I figured I'd have all my legal, dental, and medical needs met by my children, saving office visit charges. My visions of their futures were sidetracked as the teenage years kicked in and they chose other interests. I shed many tears over my lost desires for them, for their vibrant talent going untapped. I finally realized something important. My dreams were not their dreams. Their choices were not mine. So I gave up on mine.

Our verse today says that God will not turn away from the purpose he has for his people—for us. He won't give up on our addicted loved one, even when we have. He sees beyond what our eyes and hearts can see and is not afraid of the plan he has for them.

The plans may include more days in their addiction before the choice is made to lay it down. Your addict may see the inside of a jail cell while figuring out what God's recovery looks like. Although God has a divine plan, it is up to each of us to follow his leading to accomplish it. That's the hard part. But, through daily reading in his Word and communing with him through prayer, the purpose can be fully accomplished.

When you see your addict standing before a group, sharing his or her story and accepting a colored chip or keychain for a clean time milestone, you will understand God's perseverance in our lives—in your addict's life. The effort to achieve that sobriety goal is a hard-fought accomplishment. You can then say, "Well done."

DAILY PRAYER

Father, I surrender my hopes and dreams for my loved one tonight. I lay him or her before you and commit to helping my addict hear your voice and direction for his or her life. Give me wisdom as we seek your plan. Amen.

REFLECTION

What accomplishments do you have in mind for your addict? When your expectations aren't met, how do you communicate your displeasure or disappointment?

DAY 17: DESERT WANDERERS

They found grace out in the desert, these people who survived the killing. Israel, out looking for a place to rest, met God out looking for them!

Jeremiah 31:2 MSG

This is one of my favorite passages in Jeremiah 31 because it promises me divine rest. It tells me that God looks for me while I'm scurrying all over the place trying to get help for myself and my family. As you well know, chasing after your addict results in exhaustion and often proves futile.

But, in this verse we're told it was in the desert, that wilderness place, where grace was found. Who could imagine that in the midst of dealing with our addict, God shows up and extends grace, peace, and love?

On the night of October 8, 2009, I read this verse for the first time. I cried as I read that God offered grace to those who survived the sword. I crossed through the word *killing* and inserted *addiction* because that was my son's wilderness. All the years I had been going crazy with worry and fear, God was in the desert with me. He was looking for me and my family with a gift only he could give. That night changed my life, and, I believe, my son's. I committed to reading Jeremiah 30 and 31 over and over until my desert wanderer came home.

How about you? Are you stumbling through a desert, tired and thirsty, looking for a way out? I encourage you to take these two chapters to heart and believe God will extend that same grace to you and your addict. He's walking beside you in the desert, longing to give you rest.

As we live through each day with our addicts, we are survivors. We continue the battle for our children, our spouses, family members, and friends. The skirmishes will wear us out some days, but God's grace will see us through the tough places. Support groups exist to carry us through the despairing times ... those days when nothing seems right or mendable. The accountability we find at Al-Anon and Nar-Anon keep us headed in the right direction.

Although the desert is a lonely place, we don't have to walk it alone.

DAILY PRAYER

Holy Father, thank you for the desert journey I've walked with my addict. There I found your grace and rest. I consider it pure joy, for the testing of my faith develops perseverance and then wisdom. Amen.

REFLECTION

Describe some recent battles with your addict. How do you separate yourself from the chaos? Allow yourself guilt-free time to unwind and gather your thoughts.

DAY 18: THREE LITTLE WORDS

God told them, "I've never quit loving you and never will. Expect love, love, and more love."

Jeremiah 31:3 MSG

When I speak with any of my family members on the phone, I end the conversation with, "I love you." I want the last spoken words to my husband, children, mother, siblings, and others to be words of love.

I know a young man whose grandmother died unexpectedly while he was out of town. At the funeral he was overcome with grief and his sobs echoed throughout the funeral home. "I never told her I loved her," he repeated over and over. My heart broke for him because I knew he loved her. His agony over three unspoken words affected me. His laments triggered my resolve to tell my family on a daily basis those three simple words, "I love you."

Our addicts don't always make saying those words easy. Their actions and choices often make us want to say the opposite. It is easy to lash out with bitterness and hatred, but does verbally biting off their heads change their behavior?

I admit that I didn't always speak kindly to my children when they were willfully disobedient. I told them more than once, "I love you but right now I don't like you very much." In spite of what I went through, there was not a single day that I didn't love them with all my heart, and they knew it.

Commit to telling your addicted loved ones every day, "I love you." Those three words could be the magnet that draws their heart and mind to a life without drugs, alcohol, or anything else exerting control. The knowledge of being loved in spite of bad choices and wayward living can have a huge effect.

Let your addict look forward with expectation to hearing words of affirmation instead of condemnation.

DAILY PRAYER

Loving Lord, thank you for reminding me today of your love for me and my addict. I pray that I will consistently let him know how much he is loved and that I care for his well-being. Thank you for drawing me to yourself with an everlasting love. Amen.

REFLECTION

Does your addict know you love him or her? How do you show it?

DAY 19: CELEBRATING MILESTONES

Again you will take up your timbrels and go out to dance with the joyful.

Jeremiah 31:4b NIV

I did a "happy dance" when my son reached his first year anniversary of clean time in 2011. If I had a timbrel I would have shaken the daylights out of it until it could no longer make a sound. In the Old Testament, timbrels were wooden, hand-held, circular musical instruments, much like modern tambourines, with some metal pieces that clanged together when struck on the thigh or palm of the hand. Some users tied brightly colored strips of cloth to them and waved them in the air when singing or during celebrations.

The verses for today shout with joy for the great things God did for the children of Israel. Because of God's past deeds, they remembered his faithfulness, broke out the timbrels, and started dancing up a storm.

How do you celebrate your addict's milestones: 30 days, one year, or five years? Your loved one may not want a lot of attention drawn to the accomplishment, so remember to weigh his or her feelings in making your celebration decision. Maybe preparing his favorite home-cooked meal is an appropriate way to acknowledge the commitment to sobriety. A caveat to consider: your event should be alcohol free. If your addict is being released from a treatment center, he or she doesn't need to come home to a keg party or wine served with dinner, even if alcohol wasn't the controlling substance. Adjustments should be made within the family unit to boost your loved one's chances at maintaining sobriety.

We have some friends whose son struggled for years with addiction and ultimately entered a year-long treatment program. When he graduated from the program, his parents hosted an Italian feast in his honor. Aunts, uncles, cousins, and grandparents clamored around him with best wishes and prayers for a life of continued recovery. My husband and I were honored to be included on the guest list. There was much happiness in their home that night.

As a sobriety/clean time anniversary is met, it's a reminder for me that God's promises are coming true, one day at a time. The joy reminds me that Josh's life is being restored along with our family. We have many wonderful blessings over which we can shout with joy and dance with thanksgiving.

Shouting for joy is a relief after many nights of wailing in sadness.

DAILY PRAYER

Joyous Father, thank you for singing over me with joy every day. Restore that joy in my heart as I pray for my addict tonight. Let him know I take great pleasure in him. Amen.

REFLECTION

Do you acknowledge the milestones? Describe how you and your addict celebrate sobriety landmarks.

DAY 20: BUILD A STRONG FOUNDATION

> *You'll go back to your old work of planting vineyards on the Samaritan hillsides, and sit back and enjoy the fruit—oh, how you'll enjoy those harvests.*
>
> **Jeremiah 31:5 MSG**

Normalcy is a small word that becomes smaller and smaller as addiction takes over the family. The simple act of preparing dinner and gathering around the table often crumbles into scream-fests of anger. Dinner alone in your bedroom—where it is quiet and safe—becomes the new normal.

Our scripture today describes the period of time after God had restored Israel to their homeland. The farmers performed their routine activities of planting vineyards and enjoying the harvest. They did what families do to take care of one another, and these routines brought great joy to everyone. Their lives returned to normal.

Has normalcy been restored in your family? I pray it has. It may take a while for a noticeable level of regularity to segue into your home. If your addict has been in active addiction for years, it is unrealistic to expect a quick return to customary family dynamics. Each small step in that direction is a good step. Each one builds upon the next until there is a solid base upon which your family foundation is built.

Consistent routines and structure establish security. Family members know what to expect. Order replaces disorder. For example, the addict will attend meetings on a regular basis. The family will support the addict's commitment to recovery by encouraging attendance. Twelve Step groups for family members provide similar bases for the hope and strength the addict receives at meetings, and participation is encouraged. Attending these meetings encourages growth and understanding of the recovery process for the addict and the family.

Normal. It's a small word and a welcomed replacement for chaos.

DAILY PRAYER

Lord of order, bless my home with your presence tonight. Restore the desire for the regular, mundane events of our lives. In the sameness of routine may we find rest for our weary souls. Amen.

REFLECTION

Have addictive behaviors displaced your family traditions? How can you restore them?

DAY 21: "THOSE PEOPLE"

See, I will bring them from the ends of the earth. Among them will be the blind and the lame, expectant mothers and women in labor; a great throng will return.

Jeremiah 31:8 NIV

In some circles, addicts are modern-day lepers, the outcasts of society. Until my children's dalliance with drugs and alcohol and my son's eventual addiction, I harbored unkind attitudes toward "those people." I didn't associate with them because they weren't like me.

Josh met some of those people at a homeless shelter in Tampa. A bed became available for him at Manna House, a men's treatment program sponsored by Metropolitan Ministries. As we sat in the lobby waiting to meet with a counselor, he turned to me and said, "Mom, I'm not like these people. I don't belong here."

"No, you're wrong, these are now your people. Your choices made them your new friends, and you do belong here."

As he progressed in the program, we attended monthly family picnics hosted by the ministry. I met many of the residents and established rapport with several of the men. I brought desserts to the picnics and became known as "Mama Cosby." The picnics reinforced my belief that my son was no different from them; their addictions erased class distinctions.

During Josh's stay, we celebrated Thanksgiving lunch at Metropolitan Ministries. I was stripped of my self-righteousness as

I sat among the homeless, the presumed dregs of society. It was one of the best Thanksgivings I've ever celebrated because I realized that we are all part of God's family, bumps and warts included.

Look for ways to reach out to the needy in your community, extending the hand of grace. Volunteer at a feeding ministry and meet some of the presumed outcasts. Pay back the kindness someone extended to your loved one when he was in need. Find ways in your community to assist those who made some detours on their life's journey, keeping in mind someone, somewhere may be helping your loved one.

DAILY PRAYER

Father of the down and out, give me eyes to see your children as you see them. Fill my heart with compassion and help me to bind up the brokenhearted, to proclaim freedom for the captives, and to release prisoners from darkness that holds them bound. Amen.

REFLECTION

Who do you view as the most needy people in society? Do you lend assistance to the down-and-out in your community?

DAY 22: STUMBLING ALONG

I will lead them beside streams of water on a level path where they will not stumble, because I am Israel's father, and Ephraim is my firstborn son.

Jeremiah 31:9b NIV

Our home in Alabama was built in a hilly section of town. The backyard was on a steep slope leading down to a private seven-acre lake. The developers prepared a walking path around the water so the homeowners could enjoy the beauty of the setting.

Uneven ground and tree roots snaking across the path laid traps for unobservant walkers. More than once, our children faltered as they ran around the lake chasing geese or each other.

The path widened halfway around the lake into a flat, level area where we could sit and enjoy the natural splendors. The original property owners built seating for walkers to take a rest. It was a planned smooth place. Their design minimized the risk of stumbling and falling.

My house was set high above the bumpy lake path, away from tree roots and uneven ground. My desire to get to the lake needed to be stronger than the effort required to walk down the yard. If I stayed in the house and never stepped outside the door, I was on even footing. My chances of falling on the smooth surfaces of my home were small, but when I took a trip to the pathway, I put myself in the position of a potential tumble.

Isn't that the case with our addicts? We plan smooth places for their growth and enjoyment well away from the crooked, root-strewn paths of life. We may have nice houses, fancy cars, good educations—the world by a tail. Careers slide up the corporate ladder like rungs coated in Vaseline. Life is grand and all is right with the world.

Then, slowly but surely, life falls apart. The subtle slipping begins. Nights out with "the boys" or "the girls." Missed appointments. The call-outs at work. The stumbles get noticed. The smooth path to success becomes bumpy and unfriendly, not at all what you had in mind. We make excuses for our addict's behavior and become entangled in the web of deceit as well.

God longs to lead us and our addicts to streams of peaceful water. Psalm 23:1-3 (NIV) says, "The Lord is my shepherd; I shall not be in want. He makes me lie down in green pastures, he leads me beside quiet waters, he restores my soul."

Are you ready to lay aside the root-tripping path to bask in the blessings of level land?

DAILY PRAYER

Dear Father, lead me to your paths of peace and rest tonight. Thank you for the bumpy road that leads to the smooth pasture. Thank you for your guidance. Amen.

REFLECTION

With the perspective of time, how do you view your stumbles?

DAY 23: BACK IN THE FOLD

He who scattered Israel will gather them and will watch over his flock like a shepherd.

Jeremiah 31:10b NIV

Sheep need a shepherd to keep them safe from predators and sometimes from themselves. They are naturally followers. When one changes directions, the others tag along behind, even to the point of going over a cliff.

Jesus is our spiritual shepherd who gently guides us on a safe path. Sometimes we stray from his voice and follow the world into potentially dangerous places. That's how I felt on many occasions in dealing with our children's misbehaviors. My parental focus drifted, and my attention was redirected on my career, the church, or their drama. Some days my toes gripped the edge of an emotional precipice.

At night, shepherds gather the sheep into a pen, sometimes fashioned out of logs and stones. The entry to the enclosure remains open so the shepherd lies down in front of the gate to keep the sheep in and predators out. The picture is symbolic of Jesus laying down his life for his sheep—for you and me.

Our children or spouses scatter themselves by their choices to use drugs, alcohol, or other addictive behaviors. They run around with no sense of direction because they wander away from the shepherd's watchful care. A lone sheep risks attack. With no others close by to stand with him against the enemy, he must return to the herd or be lost.

Josh lost fourteen friends to drug overdoses, alcohol-related accidents and other complications by the time he was twenty years old. Unbelievable statistics for such a young population! More of his friends had died than I lost from my high school class by the time of our fortieth reunion. Many of these young people did not have the protection of a shepherd in their families; therefore, they were easy targets for the predators of drugs, alcohol, and addiction.

The beauty of God's grace is that even though we are scattered, running around chasing our tails, he gently brings us back into the fold.

DAILY PRAYER

Shepherd Father, thank you gathering me into the sheepfold. Watch over my lamb tonight and protect him from the enemy. Amen.

REFLECTION

What is a sheep's greatest need? In what ways are you a shepherd for your family? How can you improve your shepherding skills?

DAY 24: WHAT'S IT WORTH?

For the Lord will ransom Jacob and redeem them from the hand of those stronger than they.

Jeremiah 31:11 NIV

The *Merriam-Webster Dictionary* defines *ransom* as, "something paid or demanded for the freedom of a captive." In today's scripture verse, God said he would pay the price for his children.

As family members of an addict, we are familiar with ransoms and debts. We know what it's like to be strapped financially because our addict blew the grocery money on drugs, gambling, or life-controlling behaviors. We share that sinking feeling when money is paid to a lawyer to defend a DUI charge. We cringe at the invoice from the treatment center. "It costs how much to get her clean and sober?"

We ask, "How will it end? When will it end? Will it end?"

The second key word in this verse is *redeem*. I love that word. As I've walked the recovery journey, the word redeem has resonated in my heart. The *Merriam-Webster Dictionary* contains several components of the definition: "to recover (property) by discharging an obligation, to ransom, free or rescue by paying a price, to free from the consequences of sin, to convert into something of value."

For me, redemption means converting someone from damaged to valuable—beauty from ashes.

It's not always easy to believe this radical change can happen for our addicts. So much water has passed over, under, and through the dam. They've broken many promises, told many lies. To think any good can ever come from them doesn't seem possible. But it can.

Redemption is a process that requires hard work and commitment. It means gritting your teeth and keeping your mouth shut while your addicted loved one figures things out on his or her own, and letting consequences play out to their natural conclusion. It means waiting on God to do his job.

Wait expectantly for restoration and marvel at God's redeeming handiwork.

DAILY PRAYER

Father of restoration, thank you for the work you began in my loved one. Thank you that you will see it through to completion. Quiet my anxious spirit when I forget that your timing is not the same as mine. Amen.

REFLECTION

In what ways do you feel like your family has been kidnapped and held for ransom by addiction?

DAY 25: TAKE ACTION

> *Young women will dance and be happy, young men and old men will join in. I'll convert their weeping into laughter, lavishing comfort, invading their grief with joy.*
>
> **Jeremiah 13:13 MSG**

Today's scripture contains three important action words: *convert*, *lavish*, and *invade*. Each one has a place in the recovery journey.

Convert means to turn from one belief to another, to transform or change. That sums up what is happening—and what must happen—for our addicts and our families. Our belief systems must be transformed for our loved ones to succeed in recovery. By attending Twelve-Step meetings, both the addict and the family member will learn techniques to understand addiction, innovative ways to have fun with family and friends, and fresh methods to cope with stressful situations. Insights gathered from fellow travelers on this journey prove invaluable when temptations arise. The belief that "one drink won't matter" or "I can take a pill this one time" will be confronted in these group settings, and hopefully you and your addict will adopt enlightened attitudes.

The second action word is *lavish*. The word conjures mental images of abundance, of having more than I need. It actually means expending or bestowing profusely, marked by excess. In our verse today, God promised the children of Israel he would profusely bestow comfort on them. They had been in Babylonian captivity for many years and had been mistreated. They lost their possessions, their lands, and their houses. God offers them comfort, freedom from pain, trouble or anxiety.

Sounds good, doesn't it? God extends that same promise to you and me. He wants to generously pour peace into our spirits, and to relieve the anxiety that feels stuck like Velcro to our hearts and minds.

Invade is the third action word. I often felt like my home had been invaded by an alien in the form of my son and daughters. Can I get a witness? Invade means to enter for conquest or plunder, to encroach upon. God wants to invade—plunder from our hearts—the grief and sadness that weighs us down. He invites us to give up the heartache caused by our loved ones' behaviors. I like the sound of that.

Let today be one of action. Allow God and others to transform your beliefs. Permit him to lavish his comfort on you and to invade your sadness with joy.

DAILY PRAYER

Father of action, today I choose to open myself to receive your way of thinking. I choose freedom from pain and anxiety, and an invasion of holy joy! Amen.

REFLECTION

Describe what joy looks like in your life.

DAY 26: THEY WILL RETURN

> *A voice is heard in Ramah, mourning and great weeping, Rachel weeping for her children and refusing to be comforted, because they are no more. Restrain your voice from weeping and your eyes from tears, for your work will be rewarded, declares the Lord. They will return from the land of the enemy.*
>
> **Jeremiah 31:15-16 NIV**

The first time I read these verses, I wept uncontrollably. I crossed through *Rachel* and wrote *Sharron.* I marked out *Ramah* and wrote the city where I live. Those verses were mine.

I read them to my son. I made copies and mailed them and sent texts to him with the verses while he was in a treatment center. He knew I meant business. I wanted my captive back from enemy territory. "Mom, I'm getting Jeremiah 31:15-16 tattooed on my back," Josh threatened after another reminder of the verses' message.

Much like the Israelites, my family was fractured and divided. Tension at family events was so thick it could be sliced and served like a piece of chocolate cake. We continued in our misery until Josh left town for a treatment center. At times I didn't know if we, or he, would ever be whole again. But, each time I read my verses, I knew that one day my son would return from the land of his chosen exile. It took the Israelites seventy years to return to their homeland, but God kept his word. I knew, one way or another, he would keep his promise to me.

I encourage you to do the same for your loved one. Write your name in place of Rachel's name and your city's name. Own these verses and memorize them. On the occasions when your addict stumbles and you feel doubt creeping in like a black cloud, pray them aloud, reminding yourself of this incredible promise from your heavenly Father.

Twelve-Step meetings are famous for one-line sayings. One of my favorites is, "Time takes time." I've learned over the last three years that recovery is truly one day at a time. I can't pin a date on when recovery ends, for it never ends, and it happens best on a daily basis. God didn't say how long it would take for Rachel's children to come home, just that they would.

Trust him at his word.

DAILY PRAYER

Lord of the future, thank you for your promise to bring my loved one home. I will trust you with the date. Keep my eyes focused on the truth as I hide your word in my heart. Amen.

REFLECTION

Do you ever refuse comfort? Is it sometimes easier to cry and moan than to believe change can happen?

DAY 27: OUR FRAGILE HOPE

So there is hope for your descendants, declares the Lord. Your children will return to their own land.

Jeremiah 31:17 NIV

Hope keeps dreams alive. Hope provides mothers, fathers, husbands, wives, and children with the assurance of a better tomorrow. It is a divine promise.

The verses preceding today's scripture talks about Rachel crying for her children, fearful that she would not see them again. They had been captured by the Babylonians and taken far from their homeland. God heard her mourning and told her to stop crying and dry her tears for her children would come home from enemy territory.

I know that feeling, do you?

As my son began the recovery process in 2010, tiny sparks of hope brought light to the darkness in my heart and my mind. I hoped his attempts at sobriety would be successful. I anticipated a different outcome this time. I longed for an altered ending from previous attempts at getting clean. Hope was all I had left.

Many mothers I've met echo the same sentiment for their son or daughter. I recently met a lady at a conference, and we shared stories about our sons. She ended our conversation by saying, "I sure hope he 'gets it' this time. I don't think I can go through all this again." Her son had been arrested and spent several months in a county jail. During that time, he detoxed and began reading his Bible and praying. He came out clean and saying all the right things, the things she wants to hear. She prays the change in him is the real deal. Hope is all she has left.

What do we do when our fragile hope lies dashed on the floor of relapse ... of overdose? How do we process the feelings of despair when our sliver of hope for a better future evaporates into thin air?

We return—even if on our hands and knees—to the One who has the plan for our loved one safe in his hands. We remind our heavenly Father of the promise to restore and redeem. And we keep on hoping.

Each new day stretches wide with the promise of hope and expectation for a different beginning for our addicts. The moon's glow mirrors our excitement as another day ends well with sobriety intact.

Repeated daily successes increase the chances that our addicts come home full of hope and promises for a new life.

DAILY PRAYER

Lord of hope, thank you for the promises you've planted in my heart. I love you and wait with expectancy to see your plan unfold. Amen.

REFLECTION

Hope looks different to each of us. What do you hope for your loved one? Your grandchildren?

DAY 28: A NEW WAY OF DOING LIFE

I've heard the contrition of Ephraim. Yes, I've heard it clearly, saying, "You trained me well. You broke me, a wild yearling horse, to the saddle. Now put me, trained and obedient to use."

Jeremiah 31: 18 MSG

I'm not an animal trainer by any stretch of the imagination, but I know enough from watching the "Dog Whisperer" and the "Horse Whisperer" that repetition and rewards are effective teaching aids.

Too bad we can't lead our addict into a corral, whip in hand, and beat them into submission, right? If we're honest, that's what we'd like to do some days. The frustration mounts until emotions erupt and explode all over the place.

But what do we do when our addict is contrite—deeply regretful—for his or her actions? We begin a fresh approach of "doing life." Addiction coaching is double-edged: the addict learns sober methods of living and coping with situations, and the family learns different ways of responding. Both sides yearn for redirection.

I'm told the key to breaking in a horse to receive a saddle is to run him around and around the corral, bit in his mouth and the rein connected to the headpiece. The horse grows accustomed to the repetition of the movement, the tension of the mouth bit, and the weight of the saddle until he comes to realize he's being trained for a greater purpose.

The greater purpose for our addicts is to live a clean and sober life in service to others. They don't attend meetings to hoard the information for themselves. The Twelfth step in NA says, "Having had a spiritual awakening as the result of these steps, we tried to carry this message to addicts, and to practice these principles in all our affairs" (*NA Basic Text*, page 49). For alcoholics, the step is the same except use the word *alcoholics* in place of *addicts*. Once an addict has worked the steps, trained, and armed him or herself with recovery tools, he or she is ready to share with the newcomer the concept of recovery. That's the spirit of Twelve-Step groups—take the message of sobriety to one who is struggling.

Encourage your addict to use the Twelve-Step training to carry the message forward as their wills and desires are corralled into submission.

DAILY PRAYER

Lord of trainers, thank you for gently leading my loved one around life's corral. With bit and bridle in hand, you are leading him to a safe, productive place, to those who will help him grow and encourage others. Amen.

REFLECTION

Is your addict's will or spirit broken? How can you help mend it and guide your loved one to serve others?

DAY 29: STEPS TO RESTORATION

Restore me, and I will return, because you are the LORD my God.

Jeremiah 31:18b NIV

Have you ever restored a piece of furniture? The process requires the proper products, tools, and patience. The refinisher begins by removing old, chipped paint. Then he uses the right grade of sandpaper to scrape or rub at the former color, leaving a smooth surface ready to accept a new coat of paint or varnish.

Once the surface is stripped and dust-free, the craftsman looks for little nicks in the wood, places scarred or dented from years of use. He spreads wood putty on those places to restore the shape of the wood. Sometimes more sanding is needed to achieve complete evenness on the wood's surface. The final step brings the project to life. A coat of paint or varnish transforms an old worn-out piece of furniture into a new furnishing, something to be proud of.

Each step is crucial to the next one. Waiting for the first coat to dry takes patience. If a second coat is applied too soon, the end result is a bumpy surface.

Restoring a family also requires the proper tools, products, and patience. Resurfacing hurt feelings and filling in holes in relationships can take many hours of deliberate work, often through a counselor's guidance. Trust in your addict must be rebuilt, layer upon layer, until it becomes like new. Keep in mind that restoring trust is a lengthy, arduous process requiring enormous amounts of patience and love.

Today's scripture reveals the desire for restoration is in the heart of the one who strayed. The process will not be completed in one fell swoop. Addiction doesn't happen overnight and neither does restoration. You long for the day when your addict turns his or her life around and broken relationships are renewed.

Well-meaning family members often badger their loved one into treatment or recovery. You want the insanity to stop. But unless your addict takes the first step to sobriety your prodding proves futile. Until my son wanted sobriety for himself, not to please our family and get us off his back, his efforts failed time and time again.

Recovery restores the sheen of relationships.

DAILY PRAYER

Father, thank you for restoration and the patience to wait for its unfolding in my family. Bless my loved one today as layers of the past are rubbed away by the touch of your Holy Spirit. Smooth and soothe the rough places. Amen.

REFLECTION

What's your definition of restore? How can you restore your relationship with your addict?

DAY 30: TURNAROUND TIME

After I strayed, I repented.

Jeremiah 31:19a NIV

My traditional religious upbringing defined repentance as a 180° turn in the direction one is headed. If people were walking in sin—drinking, drugs, lying, premarital sex—and then made a profession of faith in Jesus as their Savior, their lives would take an about-face, and they would head in a new route of living.

The *Merriam-Webster Dictionary's* definition is to turn from sin and to resolve to reform one's life; to feel sorry for something done.

Both definitions fit today's scripture verse. Our loved ones have strayed—some farther than others. The wandering road led down paths fraught with danger. Some changed geographical locations. For many, the journey ended in a prison cell. Their choices led away from those who love them.

When our son was immersed in his addiction, he drifted far from his childhood teachings. He engaged in activities that he knew were wrong. One October night in 2009, I woke to find Josh in one of our spare bedrooms sobbing. He said, "Mom, what have I done? What have I gotten myself into? This is the worst stuff I've ever messed with. I'm so sorry." I held him, and we cried together.

His questions were double-sided. The choices he made to feed his addiction were worse than ever. The people he associated with were on a deeper level of bad. Painkillers gripped his mind and body more tightly than the drugs he used before. This time, he was in real trouble.

That night was the beginning of his turnaround. Four months passed before he took the about-face steps, but the seed was planted, and the desire for genuine repentance took root.

Has your addicted loved one sunk to his or her lowest level yet? This realization is referred to as "hitting bottom." Everyone's bottom is at a different depth. It is hard to know when he will reach the end of himself and make a decision to make life change.

Hang on to your addict. Cling to the hope that repentance is possible. When he comes to the point of recognition and remorse, life change happens.

DAILY PRAYER

Father of turnarounds, bless my loved one today. Make straight the path before him, the one that leads to you. Amen.

REFLECTION

What is your definition of repent? What will that look like for your addict?

DAY 31: THE "AHA" MOMENT

After I came to understand, I beat my breast.

Jeremiah 31:19b NIV

Do you remember the V8 juice commercials where the actor smacks himself on the forehead with the heel of his hand and says, "I could have had a V8!?" That is a scripted "aha" moment of realization. In the actor's case, he realizes there is a better choice of drink than a soda or coffee.

What about our addicts? What about us as the family members of addicts? Do you recall your "V8 moment" when you comprehended your loved one had a serious problem?

My first one came when Josh was sixteen years old. He had missed four days of school in one week. He left for school each day, but he never made it. He skipped school, drank alcohol, and smoked marijuana. While my husband was out of the country working, I arranged for Josh to go into treatment. When Dan returned, we took Josh to his new temporary home. We pulled into the driveway and Josh said, "This looks like a place you come to stay." He did—for twenty-eight days.

The week of his misbehavior left me with an utter sense of helplessness. The seriousness of his drinking descended like a steel cage around my heart. Sixteen years old and entering a rehab center for alcohol and drug abuse. How did we get to that place of need?

Several years passed before Josh had his "aha" moment. He wept as the light bulbs came on in his head, and he acknowledged he was in deep, deep trouble. He didn't beat his breast, but he wept uncontrollably as his past, present, and future crushed him like a steamroller. The enormity of his addiction fell heavily on both of us as he made tough decisions about getting help.

When your addicted loved one reaches his or her moment of clarity, how will you respond? Visualize it and mentally prepare responses. For instance, you may want to research available treatment centers so that when your addict throws in the towel, you are ready with immediate solutions. "Strike while the iron is hot," as the old saying goes.

Accept the fact that our "aha" moment will probably not coincide with our addicts' burst of "Oh my God, I'm in trouble" awakening. Regrettably, we have to wait on them to have the revelation—to beat their breast or take action.

DAILY PRAYER

Dear Lord of clarity and truth, thank you for shining your light on areas that need attention. Thank you for the courage to make decisions, many times painful and difficult. Thank you for helping my loved one to see the destructive path and correct his steps. Amen.

REFLECTION

Have you had an "aha" moment concerning your family's situation? Write it down and reflect on what brought you to the revelation.

DAY 32: SHAME AND BLAME

I was ashamed and humiliated because I bore the disgrace of my youth.

Jeremiah 31:19c NIV

Shame and humiliation often walk alongside fear and worry when living with an addict. As family members, we pick up the debris left behind by inappropriate behaviors, figuratively and literally. Broken doors and windowpanes require repair and perhaps an explanation to a landlord . Neighbors spread gossip after witnessing the response to a 911 call to your house.

Thankfully, that was not our family's story. We never had physical damage to mend, but there were, and are, emotional wounds that need to heal. Relationships between friends suffer because of our addicts' behaviors.

The neighborhood where we built our first Florida home consisted of upper middle class families with lofty behavior expectations. When our teenagers' involvement with the alcohol and drug scene spilled into the vacant lot beside our home, our family became the bane of the neighborhood. Once-friendly neighbors turned their backs on us. Party invitations ceased. I was hurt and humiliated by the reactions of others to my children's misbehaviors.

Years after we moved, I saw a former neighbor. She stopped me in a shopping center parking lot. "I'm so sorry, Sharron."

"For what?"

With tear-filled eyes she said, "For talking about you and your family when your kids were messing around." She went on to tell me about her sons' drug usage and arrests. My heart broke with hers. Ironically, the tide had turned, and her family had become the neighborhood outcasts.

We often don't know what's happening behind the closed doors of our neighbors' homes. Pain and problems may surround a family, but shame and humiliation prevent them from seeking help. Offering to listen to a mother's lament or a father's anguish go a long way in instilling hope. To know someone cares is important when we feel hopeless.

Recognize signs of weariness in friends and family members. Remembering your own embarrassment and pain, reach out to comfort a hurting family.

DAILY PRAYER

Dear Father, thank you for taking my shame and creating a crown of your glory and grace. May I remember the pain of humiliation and offer comfort and care when I see another's wounds caused by their addicted loved one. Amen.

REFLECTION

Recall some humiliating incidents caused by your addict's behavior. Can you forgive them for their actions? Describe what forgiveness looks like for you and your addict.

DAY 33: STOP, LOOK AND LISTEN!

Set up road signs; put up guideposts. Take note of the highway, the road that you take.

Jeremiah 31:21 NIV

Stop signs and traffic lights regulate traffic to prevent accidents. But what happens when a driver ignores the bright red stop sign or tries to make it through a yellow caution light? Sometimes a wreck occurs, causing avoidable injuries and property damage.

Not far from my home, some teenagers removed a stop sign from a heavily traveled intersection. An innocent truck driver went through the intersection and rammed into a car, instantly killing the driver. The teens were located and criminally charged with the driver's death. To them, removing the sign was a harmless prank; to the automobile driver it had a deadly outcome.

Road signs promote road safety. The same is true for personal safety from life-altering behaviors, such as drugs, alcohol, gambling and unprotected sex. Our laws set guidelines and or parameters for behaviors to protect us and those around us. Legislators didn't arbitrarily select twenty-one years as the legal age to purchase alcohol. There is medical and scientific evidence to support that age range. The human brain continues to grow and develop until ages twenty-one to twenty-five. If alcohol or other substances are introduced at an earlier age, permanent damage can occur.

In today's scripture, Jeremiah reminded the Israelites to put up road signs and guideposts so they would remember where they had been. The same reminder applies today. Recall the road you've traveled with your addicted loved one. Your guidepost can be as simple as a calendar marked with a sobriety date. It becomes a constant reminder of the path to a clean and healthy lifestyle.

Road signs and streetlights are not to punish a driver; they are a means of safety. Parental boundaries and guidelines are to protect our loved ones from harm. Respect them for what they are.

DAILY PRAYER

Dear Lord, thank you for stop signs and red lights. Thank you that my loved one is learning to stop, look and listen at each of them. I'm grateful for the green lights you've posted along his road to recovery. Amen.

REFLECTION

Have you ever run a stop sign or red traffic light? Did you get ticketed? What did you learn from the experience?

DAY 34: THE RELAPSE ISSUE

Come back, dear virgin Israel, come back to your hometowns. How long will you flit here and there, indecisive? How long before you make up your fickle mind?

Jeremiah 31:21b-22a MSG

Relapse is part of recovery. It occurs for many reasons and lasts varying lengths of time.

Josh entered treatment in November of 2009 and had three or four weeks of clean time under his belt. Then, out of the blue, he was knocked down by a gallbladder attack. After surgery he returned to the treatment center with a bottle of pain pills. He relapsed, again, was discharged, and moved back home.

Through no fault of his own, his attempt at sober living was disrupted and prescription pain medicine refueled the flames of his addiction. His usage skyrocketed before he reentered the treatment facility two months later.

Our addicts think they can flit along the edges of the drug and alcohol scenes, toying with using again. Josh tried the party scene, drinking diet sodas, but eventually gave in to the desire to join the crowd and returned to alcohol. Drinking precipitated drugs, and before long, he relapsed. This pattern of relapse and sobriety occurred several times before February 18, 2010.

Our scripture for today poses the question, "How long before you make up your fickle mind?" How long will our addicts continue in their addictive behaviors? Until they get sick and tired of being sick and tired. Until they are arrested and are forced into sobriety. It is hard to accept that only our addicts can answer the question, "How long?"

The obvious way to avoid relapse is by "doing the next right thing" in Twelve-Step parlance. Regular attendance at AA, NA, Celebrate Recovery, or other Twelve-Step meetings is crucial to maintaining a sober life. A job change may be necessary to disassociate from substance using co-workers. An adjustment in persons, places, and things promotes sustained recovery. We can help them by educating ourselves on relapse prevention and by providing support.

Be prepared for relapse. Watch for old behaviors and intervene before a misstep occurs. Be aware of triggers such as music (for Josh it was techno and reggae), carrying large amounts of cash, and hanging out with old friends. Even smells can trigger a relapse. Learn your addict's triggers and be proactive in helping to avoid them.

Flirting with old lifestyles puts our loved ones in the crosshairs of relapse. Encourage a clean break.

DAILY PRAYER

Dear Father of second chances, thank you for restoring my loved one when he stumbles and falls. I pray that his days of fickle, flirty decisions become years of solid, God-filled, unwavering choices. Amen.

REFLECTION

Has your addict experienced a relapse? Write down how you coped and what your loved one did following the relapse.

DAY 35: REST FOR THE WEARY

I will refresh the weary and satisfy the faint.
Jeremiah 31:25 NIV

Is there rest for the weary—for us, the family members of addicts? Today's scripture tells us there is.

Jeremiah records in verse 26 that after the Lord said, "I will refresh the weary and satisfy the faint," he awoke, and his sleep had been pleasant. That was not my testimony for several years. Sweet, calming sleep avoided me like kids playing dodge ball. Ragged thoughts of Josh's addiction bounced from one side of my mind to another. From one hour to the next, I never slept long enough to get much-needed rest.

Jesus said to a crowd in Matthew 11:28-29a NIV, "Come to me, all you who are weary and burdened, and I will give you rest. Take my yoke upon you and learn from me." What can we learn from Jesus about rest? He knew the people were living under political, financial, and religious pressures, and they were exhausted. He offered them love, healing, and peace, not a life of leisure.

He makes the same offer to you and me, to those of us dragging our feet through each day, weary from our fights and fears. How do we appropriate this rest? By believing in the One who makes the offer.

I had read scripture verses about rest and sleep for many years, but until I found Jeremiah 30 and 31, and truly believed God would and could restore my family, I tossed and turned night after night.

I fretted and worried by day, not confident the offer of peace and rest was mine.

I encourage you to immerse yourself in God's Word, his love letter to his children. Read the Psalms and allow the timeless words to soothe your spirit and comfort you in dark and doubting moments. Proverbs provides guidance for leading your family to godliness and right living.

As you go to bed tonight, direct your thoughts to dwell on the positive qualities of the addict in your life. Imagine the days when addiction will be a point of reference in the past and not a daily occurrence or a source of pain. Shut your eyes and dream of the better days ahead, and may your sleep be sweet.

DAILY PRAYER

Sweet Lord of rest, sleep and dreams, I thank you that my sleep is sweet; that your all-seeing eyes never close on me and my loved one. You watch my chest rise and fall and love me. You love my addict too. Amen.

REFLECTION

Does sleep elude you? Describe your exhaustion and how it affects your family. How do you refresh yourself?

DAY 36: WHEN LIFE IS A NIGHTMARE

Just then I woke up and looked around—what a pleasant and satisfying sleep!

Jeremiah 31:26 MSG

Vivid dreams seep into our conscious, awake selves. The images don't vanish when our eyes open. They tag along in our minds as we go about the routines of our day. We can't shake the vividness of the dream.

The reality of our experiences with our addict seems nightmarish at times. We can't dispel the sense of urgency of late-night phone calls or the sinking feeling in the pit of our stomachs when we realize items in the house are missing. We wonder how our family ended up with this mess we call life.

How do we process these feelings and emotions?

Start by admitting your powerlessness over the situation and that your life is unmanageable. This is the first step both the addict and his or her family must take on the road to recovery and wholeness. Dr. Phil, the television talk-show host and former psychologist, often says that you can't change what you don't acknowledge. Until we own the problems in our families, we will stay trapped in our nightmares.

The second step is to seek professional help or attend a Twelve-Step group meeting. A professional counselor will assess the situation and determine what kind of treatment is necessary to help the addict and the family make appropriate lifestyle changes. Outpatient therapy may be sufficient to get your loved one on the path to recovery. For some, inpatient treatment may be required depending on the drugs, length of time used, and other factors. Twelve-Step groups lend emotional and moral support to the addict in ways family members cannot. The family will receive help by attending Al-Anon or Nar-Anon meetings.

Remember, the nightmare of addiction won't end overnight. You may wake up morning after morning in a cold sweat or shedding tears. The good news is that assistance and support are available. You don't have to fight the terrors alone.

You will wake up one morning and exclaim with Jeremiah, "What a pleasant and satisfying sleep." You will be satisfied with the work and progress of your addicted loved one and your family, and the dreadful dreams will fade into the sea of forgetfulness.

DAILY PRAYER

Dear Father, I thank you for being my sandman, the one who brings sweet sleep and pleasant dreams. Watch over my loved one tonight, dusting him with contentment, wholeness, and rest. Amen.

REFLECTION

Does your life sometimes feel like a bad dream? Describe the good days that offset the bad.

DAY 37: THE BLAME GAME

When that time comes you won't hear the old proverb anymore, Parents ate the green apples, and their children got the stomachache. No, each person will pay for his own sin. You eat green apples; you're the one who gets sick.

Jeremiah 31:29-30 MSG

It is easy to blame our addict for every family issue. We may think, *if she would just behave. If he would just quit drinking. If he would just respect his curfew and come home on time.* If. If. If.

After many years of dealing with our son's addiction and the attendant problems it created, my husband finally admitted to himself and then to me, "Many times I thought that if Josh would clean up his act and behave, we wouldn't have any problems." He placed the blame for our situation squarely on our son's young shoulders. He never verbalized that to Josh, but Josh was the unspoken family scapegoat.

The reverse is also true. Our addicts blame us, as parents, siblings or spouses for their woes.

"If you had been better parents."

"If you hadn't hounded me to make more money."

"If you weren't always telling me what to do."

"If you didn't have to have a new house."

If. If. If.

The verses for today address personal responsibility. There was a proverb in Jeremiah's day that said, "Parents eat the green apples and their children get the stomachache." It meant the consequences of the parents trickled down to the children. Jeremiah told the Israelites when they were restored to their land there would be no more trickle-down effect. Each person would bear responsibility for their own behaviors; you eat green apples, you get the stomachache.

Personal accountability for one's action is a worthy lesson to teach our children from an early age. By the time they reach the vulnerable middle-school years, they should understand owning the consequences for their behaviors. When we coddle them, and enable them to avoid penalties, we hurt them in the long run.

Hurling blame at one another does nothing to resolve discord within the family. Acknowledge your role, accept appropriate liability for the situation, and encourage other family members to do the same. Mutual accountability and responsibility go a long way in healing relationships and finding solutions to the family's problems.

DAILY PRAYER

Dear Lord, help me to recognize my role in our family's problems. Embolden me to say, "I'm sorry." May my example cause others to see and accept their portion of responsibility in the situation. In faith, I thank you for the healing that will take place. Amen.

REFLECTION

It's easy to point the finger of blame for the family's problems at your addict. List ways family members blame your loved one for the family's problems.

DAY 38: WHAT'S THE PLAN?

For I know the plans I have for you, declares the Lord, plans to prosper you and not to harm you, plans to give you hope and a future.

Jeremiah 29:11 NIV

Winston Churchill said, "He who fails to plan is planning to fail." The saying is often quoted at high school and college graduation ceremonies. Corporate executives use it in pep talks to inspire employees. The crux of the statement is that we need a plan, a direction to our lives; otherwise we flounder and fail.

Do we plan our family's future the way a commander would strategize a military strike? Is there a family board meeting during which the future is detailed? Probably not. We didn't gather as a family and discuss the direction we'd like to see our family take. We were lax in guiding our children in career paths. That's not to say that if we had a family blueprint the outcome would be different. Our children could, and did, make their own choices, but at least some attempts to plan could have been made.

What about your family? Do you have a clear picture of how your family functions or how you would like it to function? Are there mutually agreed-upon goals each family member can achieve?

Today's verse is about God's plan for Israel. It was a good plan that would see them safely back to their homeland. But, the preceding verses are often overlooked. God tells the Israelites they will be in captivity for seventy years. During that time they were to plant crops, build houses, and settle down. They were to continue routine living despite their desperate situations. Then, when the time was right, He would fulfill His promises to prosper and to offer hope and a future.

In that context, as a family walking through addiction and recovery, I see that I'm to do what is necessary to live in the current situation with my addicted loved one. I will learn about addiction and recovery. I will support my son in his efforts. Then, in God's time, He will pour out the promises He has in store for us, promises that bring hope and a future.

DAILY PRAYER

God of eternal plans, thank you for the direction you have for the life of each one in my family. As I yield my heart to you, reveal your perfect plan in your heavenly time. Open my eyes to see what you have in store. I entrust my children to your calendar of events. Amen.

REFLECTION

What plans have you made for your addict? For your family? For yourself? How have your changed them because of the addiction journey?

DAY 39: THE BAD APPLE EFFECT

Dear friend, if bad companions tempt you, don't go along with them.

Proverbs 1:10 MSG

Purchase a three-to-five-pound bag of apples, place them in a wicker basket, leave them in a cool, dark space, and watch what happens. One of the apples will begin to deteriorate. A day or two later, an apple touching against the rotten one will turn soft and brown. From that core group of rotting apples, more and more will spoil. Friends can produce the same result as a basket of rotten apples.

One of Josh's friends, whom I didn't particularly care for, came by our house one day to get him. He wasn't home yet, so this young man and I started talking. I don't remember the exact conversation, but it ended with him telling me horrible things about my son. He said I sugarcoated everything about Josh and that I wouldn't accept the fact my son was bad. I was flabbergasted at his comments. My son? Bad?

When Dan got home from work I told him about the young man's comments. After a few minutes of quiet thought he looked at me and said, "You know, our kids *are* the bad kids. We always blame their behavior on someone else, but they influence others." I knew in my heart he was right, but I didn't want to believe that my children could be *bad*.

King Solomon, the wisest man who ever lived, warned young men (it's applicable to young women as well) about the influence of friends. I like the word influence over peer pressure because many times it's the slow, steady sway of behaviors, thoughts and even music, that leads young people and adults to make unwise choices, much like apples rotting in a basket.

The book of Proverbs is loaded with admonitions to steer clear of enticing situations: alcohol, prostitutes, unethical business practices, and other areas that still affect our lives today.

Encourage your young person to weigh his or her friends' activities to avoid undue influence.

Help them recognize "bad apple" traits and steer clear of them.

DAILY PRAYER

Dear Father, the giver of wisdom, flood my mind with godly wisdom as I speak into my addict's life. May my words and deeds be flavored with your insights. Open his eyes and heart to receive your message. Amen.

REFLECTION

Does your addict understand the concept of how one bad apple spoils the whole basket? Help him understand what that means about himself and his friends.

DAY 40: WATCH OUT!

Keep vigilant watch over your heart; that's where life starts.

Proverbs 4:23 MSG

Vigilant is defined in *The Merriam Webster Dictionary* as alertly watching, especially to avoid danger. How do we do that? Does vigilance have any relevance to addiction and recovery? Yes, without a doubt.

King Solomon's admonishment or instruction to his sons was to protect their hearts—the seat of their emotions and thoughts. Another scripture says, "Listen my son, and be wise, and keep your heart on the right path." (Proverbs 23:19 NIV). Our thoughts produce our actions. A scripture in Philippians says to think on things that are true, pure, lovely, or praiseworthy (Philippians 4:8). How do we do that for ourselves and for our children in our technology-driven society?

We can limit movies, television programming, music videos and video games. Children today are exposed to much more violence and sexual content than when I was a child. In retrospect, the cartoons we watched, such as "Tom and Jerry," "Roadrunner," and even "Bugs Bunny" had violent components, but they weren't violent for violence's sake. Modern movies, video games, and music videos are violence saturated, desensitizing our children by excessive portrayals of viciousness and savagery.

The media applaud immoral behavior and portray heavy drinking and partying as acceptable, normal behaviors of teenagers and adults. As consumers, we approve it with each ticket purchase. Our children grow up thinking it's okay to get drunk and behave promiscuously. Their moral compasses are stunted, in part, because of the hedonistic overload of movies and music.

As parents, we set the standard in our homes for appropriate media choices. We can have conversations with our children about the value of feeding our hearts and minds with wholesome content. Our scripture today says from the heart springs life. King Solomon advised us to keep a vigilant watch over it. As true today as thousands of years ago, his words imply the need for constant attention in guarding one's heart. Parents face the challenge of identifying dangers in the media and taking a stand, in order to oppose the weakening or destruction of the nation's moral fiber.

Consider what your children and teenagers hear, see, and experience—the influences that penetrate their very souls. Take baby steps in refocusing the family's television, movie, and entertainment habits. Slow and steady wins the race.

DAILY PRAYER

Dear Father, guide my decisions in leading my family to think on what is lovely, pure, and pleasing to you. I ask that my loved one's heart will be softened to accept new ways of thinking and behaving. Amen.

REFLECTION

Define vigilant. How does that apply to guarding your heart?

DAY 41: AVOIDING THE SECOND GLANCE

... I noticed among the young men, a youth who lacked judgment. He was going down the street near her corner, walking along in the direction of her house ...

Proverbs 7:7-8 NIV

Recording artists Casting Crowns released a song several years ago entitled "Slow Fade." The lyrics describe the slow descent into destructive behaviors and devastating consequences. The song suggests that it's the second glance that causes thoughts to turn to lust, resulting in wrong choices. The overall message is families aren't lost in a day but over time as poor decisions accumulate. Temptations come through things touched, seen, and heard. Constant exposure to the wrong environment erodes your beliefs and corrodes actions.

The scripture for today describes a young man walking along a street near the corner where prostitutes gather. He was near the corner—not quite there yet. There was time to turn and run from the lure of the brazen women. He walked on the fringes of involvement.

Our addicted loved ones once walked on the fringes of involvement. It's called experimentation: the thrill of the first drink, cigarette or joint, even skipping school—just to see what it would be like. Some stop at the fringes. They tried it once, didn't like it, and that was the end of it.

For others, the initial experience opens the door for further involvement with drugs, alcohol, sexual acting out, pornography, and a host of other controlling behaviors. They liked the sensations and kept coming back for more and more. That phase is called the recreation phase; it becomes a regular part of their activities.

Next is the habituation phase; they depend more and more on the substance or behavior. It graduates to a physical demand and not just an emotional or psychological need.

Habituation many times develops into abuse or addiction. Users must have the drug or activity to maintain a sense of well-being. The pleasure-seeking euphoria that caught them in the web no longer is the reason they use. They use so they don't hurt. Withdrawal is painful.

And to think it all began by walking on the fringes, dabbling a little at a time, not realizing the danger lurking on the proverbial street corners. As King Solomon warned his sons of the temptations, share with your adolescents and teens the possible scenarios of abuse and addiction.

DAILY PRAYER

Dear Lord, lover of fringe walkers, open our eyes to the forces enticing our loved ones. Fill them with courage to run in the opposite direction when temptations come their way. Amen.

REFLECTION

Describe one or two areas in which you gradually shifted your moral compass.

DAY 42: LIFTING THE LOAD

Worry weighs us down; a cheerful word picks us up.

Proverbs 12:25 MSG

Worry is what keeps you up at night, flip-flopping in bed like a fish out of water. It's what eats away at your stomach lining like battery acid on a sponge. It's that chill that slithers down your spine like a melting ice cube. Worry brings a corduroy texture to your forehead when you ponder your addict's latest antic. What can we do with this worrisome worry?

Fight it every step of the way. For God-followers, we pray and ask for guidance, peace, and protection. People who lack a relationship with God muster their own strength and power.

Today's scripture suggests that a kind word lifts the heavy weight of worry. Has anyone ever spoken a kind word to you at the moment you were crushed under a boulder of worry? Momentarily, you felt revived and emotionally lighter.

When Josh was in active addiction all I did was worry about what would happen to him, and to our family. I was the proverbial basket case and didn't function too well. Three co-workers listened to my concerns and fears, wiped my tears as I sobbed out my story, and loved me through a terrible, relentless nightmare. They couldn't change the situation, but they could, and did, walk with me through that season of darkness. I am forever grateful to them.

Their encouragement buoyed my sagging spirit. They usually got a smile, if not a laugh, out of me and, for a moment, I felt better. Do you have people like that in your life? Who will hold your hand and lend an ear? Are you that kind of friend?

I also found in Jeremiah 30 and 31 words that cheered me and gave me hope. After reading these two chapters, I finally released my worries about my son's future to God's plan, and the weight was lifted. I still have days when doubts creep in. When that happens, I go straight to these two chapters and reread God's promises for restoration and redemption. Assurance from my heavenly Father drives away the root of worry.

If you don't have a friend or family member to confide in, may I suggest you locate an Al-Anon or Nar-Anon meeting and attend? You will come in contact with families with similar fears and worries, and they will offer their strength, hope, and experience. Members will say a kind word at the right time.

Reach out to others to lighten their loads. Grab the hand extended to you to find friendship and help with your burdens.

DAILY PRAYER

Dear Lord, forgive me when I worry and fret over my loved one. Help me to lean on your promises. Bring someone into my path in need of a kind word. May I be a burden lifter. Amen.

REFLECTION

What lifts your spirits when you're worried about your addict?

DAY 43: BROKEN DREAMS

Hope deferred makes the heart sick, but a longing fulfilled is a tree of life.

Proverbs 13:12 NIV

Life with an addict is a series of dashed hopes and dreams. Each stay in a treatment facility buoys the hope that this time he or she will "get it" and the cycle of addiction will end. Your addict comes out of jail clean and sober, saying all the right things, starting with, "I'm sorry. This is the last time I'll ever use." And for a few days all is well, until he or she relapses, and your reveries of a bright future go down the toilet.

Our verse for today in *The Message* says, "Unrelenting disappointment leaves you heartsick, but a sudden good break can turn life around." As the parent or spouse of an addict, we face unending disappointments. Time and time again we expect things to be different, but they aren't. Each relapse bruises our hearts and heaps misery upon misery.

Beside this verse in my Bible I wrote: "You know the longing of my heart, please fulfill it." My desire was to see my son free of addiction's bondage and all that accompanies it. I didn't date the entry, but on February 18, 2010, the yearning of my heart began to unfold. That was the date Josh entered his last treatment center, and he has remained clean and sober for more than three years.

I can tell you that a tree of life sprouted in my heart as each day stacked itself onto the next until he reached his first year of clean time. The medallion he received from his NA sponsor was as precious to me as if it had been an Olympic gold medal. I believe the work he did was as strenuous as Olympic training.

The hope for my son to be drug-free was a long time coming. It was delayed through choices Josh made that prevented a sustainable recovery. With each setback, I doubted sobriety would ever happen, but each time I rallied my spirit and started over.

The verse today offers us assurance as we love our addicts. The desires of our hearts—for our addicts to live in recovery—may be postponed, but as long as there remains a breath in their bodies the tree of life can take root and grow.

DAILY PRAYER

Dear Father of hope, thank you that dreams and longings are fulfilled in your timing and that I'm learning to yield to your timeline and not my own. Water the tree of life one day at a time to produce hardy, shade-producing foliage. Amen.

REFLECTION

Describe your heart's desires for your addict. Consider sharing them with your loved one and develop ways to make them a reality.

DAY 44: POUR IT OUT

Each heart knows its own bitterness, and no one else can share its joy.

Proverbs 14:10 NIV

A story in the New Testament tells about a woman who anointed Jesus with expensive oil poured from an alabaster jar (Matthew 26:6-13). The disciples were appalled and scolded her for wasting the precious commodity. They could have sold it and used the money to help poor people. Jesus rebuked them and praised the woman. Her gift and presentation received harsh judgment.

The alabaster box represents one's sacrifice, tears, and tough times. The box can be filled with wrong choices: divorce, addiction, abortion, and thievery. It can be loaded with gossip, envy, greed, and lust. We tuck our hurts and disappointments inside the box, trying to hide them from the world. I don't know what's in your box just as you don't know what is in mine. But God knows, and each time I offer it to him as a sacrifice, I share in his joy at my release.

While Josh was in a Tampa treatment center several years ago, we attended a concert together, and CeCe Wynan's "Alabaster Box" was performed. We both wept as the words were acted out in sign language. Josh leaned over and said to me, "Mom, nobody knows what's in my box. No one understands what I've gone through." My heart broke for him.

Our families, friends, and neighbors are often like Jesus' disciples. They ridicule us for spilling the oil of forgiveness on our addicted loved ones. "What a waste," they chide, "your energies will be better spent on someone who will appreciate you."

Do you have an alabaster box? Do you secret away bitterness, tears, and disappointments? How much would it cost you to pour them out before the Lord and allow him to accept them as a sacrifice of praise? He will replace the bitterness with joy that is special for you.

Pray for an opportunity to share your alabaster box story with your addict, allowing God to work through your transparency to provide a way to healing.

DAILY PRAYER

Dear Lord, I thank you for what's in my alabaster box. As it is broken before you, may its sweet fragrance be pleasant and honoring to you. By my example, help my loved one empty his container and receive your healing and joy. Amen.

REFLECTION

Share a story with your loved one from your alabaster box. Invite him or her to do the same.

DAY 45: RISKY BEHAVIOR

There's a way of life that looks harmless enough; look again—it leads straight to hell.

Proverbs 14:12 MSG

Now that your loved one is teetering on the brink or embroiled in an addiction, do you ever wonder if your life and theirs would be different had they not done certain things? In the beginning these choices may have seemed innocent and harmless—things that everyone does.

I beat myself up with a list of what ifs. If only I had asked my children more questions before they left the house for a night out with friends. If I had met the parents of their friends we could have agreed on acceptable behaviors. If I had asked why crushed soda cans with holes poked in them regularly littered the garage. If I had asked why cigar tobacco was all over the pool deck when my son's friends were at the house? If only I had asked, "Where are you going? With whom?"

I didn't ask the questions because I was afraid of the answers.

If I had asked, I would have discovered my son and his friends were using the soda cans as marijuana pipes. The cigars were "blunts," a cigar split open, the tobacco replaced with marijuana, then smoked.

Their unsupervised gatherings at our house appeared harmless enough, as today's scripture says, but they actually harbored behaviors and attitudes that led to deadly lifestyle choices for some. The desire to be grownup, drink, have sex, and do drugs wreaked havoc. Because of drugs and alcohol, some of them lost their lives, aborted their babies, or went to prison.

Because movies and television shows portray drinking, drugs and sex as an expected, natural part of the teen experience, this is becoming the rule rather than the exception. We excuse underage drinking by saying, "It's just what kids do. They all try it. Leave them alone; they will be fine." The media portrays cheating on spouses as acceptable. It looks harmless enough in the beginning, but the results are devastating.

As you gather information on addiction, you can confidently ask the tough questions and set appropriate boundaries. No longer excuse bad behaviors as "it's just what kids do" or "everyone is doing it," turning a blind eye and allowing them to continue on a destructive path.

Armed with information and concern, guide your loved one back onto the road of life.

DAILY PRAYER

Lord, thank you for opening my eyes to the truth of risky behaviors and choices. Give me wisdom to make right decisions and the backbone to set godly boundaries in love. Amen.

REFLECTION

What activities did your child or spouse participate in that initially appeared harmless but turned out to be dangerous?

DAY 46: FEARING THE WORST

Even in laughter the heart may ache, and joy may end in grief.

Proverbs 14:13 NIV

Relapse is to recovery like white is to rice. It is almost an expectation, particularly the first time the addict attempts to abandon the lifestyle. It's not defeatist, it's realistic.

My son first attempted recovery at age sixteen. He didn't want to be at the treatment center, but he didn't have a choice. We admitted him and left. Within two months of getting out, he was taken by ambulance to an emergency room with an overdose. That began a rollercoaster of recovery and relapse spanning fifteen years.

As our verse today says, "Even in laughter, the heart may ache." We've experienced many happy times as a family during the last few years, but a cloud of heartache hovers over my head. I wait for the other shoe to drop, wondering when the good times will end because of another relapse.

Living with an addict brings uncertainty because we are not in control. We cannot dictate their choices, but we pick up the pieces. Frustration is glued to our hearts by a disease we don't understand.

What happens when the treatment centers, support groups, counseling sessions, and Twelve Steps don't work? How do we cope with the failure? How do we process the death of our loved one because of alcohol or drug abuse? The intervals of joy during moments of clarity and sobriety can be blown to bits by one relapse and can result in death.

Loss by overdose devastates family members. Guilt and shame tear at them like rabid pit bulls gnashing and ripping apart a rooster. Joy from the clean times can be whisked away by one wrong decision. During these times our support systems rise to the occasion and carry us through the hurt.

Cherish each day as you revel in the laughter and joy of sobriety. We don't know what tomorrow holds, and our joy may end in grief. Live one day at a time with great expectancy and hope in the One who holds our loved ones in the palms of his hands.

DAILY PRAYER

Father, I place my fear of relapse at your feet. It is a possibility, but in faith I pray it's no longer a probability. Thank you that my loved one is taking steps to stay clean and sober. Thank you for your promise to bring my loved one home. Amen.

REFLECTION

How do you handle the prospect of your loved one's relapse or death by overdose?

DAY 47: SEEDS OF KINDNESS

He who oppresses the poor shows contempt for their Maker, but whoever is kind to the needy honors God.

Proverbs 14:31 NIV

We see homeless people on street corners holding their cardboard resumes: "Will work for food." "Hungry. Please help." "Veteran. Thank you & God bless."

Some people look on the homeless with contempt and disdain, refusing to donate a dollar to an outstretched hand for fear the beggar will purchase drugs or alcohol with their money. Others slip a dollar bill through half-opened car windows out of guilt, not making eye contact. Most of us assume these beggars are drunks and junkies. Sometimes, they are, but often reasons beyond their control create homelessness.

One Saturday afternoon as I waited for the traffic light to change, I saw an unkempt young man sitting on a bus stop bench. I ignored him and drove on my way when the light turned green, but I couldn't get him off my mind. I had to do something to help.

I went to a nearby McDonalds and bought a super-sized Big Mac Meal and drove back to where I had seen him, praying he would still there. He was. I pulled into the parking lot and drove close to him. Rolling down the window, I called, "Hey! I brought you some food." As he approached, I extended the bag of food and the drink. His eyes lit up like fireworks at the sight of the McDonald's bag.

Our eyes met briefly, and I said to him, "I've brought you

something to eat. God bless you, son." He thanked me, returned to his seat, and tore into the sack of food. I prayed that God would protect him and comfort his mother's heart wherever she might be.

I saw my son in that young man. I was planting seeds that day. I knew that my son could be on the streets and hungry because of the choices he was making. I wanted to believe someone would help and extend kindness to him in my absence.

As families of addicts, we can go the extra mile in offering grace and mercy to those in need. We may be the answer to a discouraged parent's prayer and someone else could be the answer to ours.

Planting seeds of kindness may reap a harvest for your loved one.

DAILY PRAYER

Sweet Lord, thank you for caring for the poor and needy. Open my eyes and heart to those around me who are hungry for a touch from you. May I be the hands of Jesus to a hurting world. Amen.

REFLECTION

How can you show kindness to the needy? Does that include your addict? Other addicts?

DAY 48: "I NEED HELP"

First pride, then the crash—the bigger the ego, the harder the fall.

Proverbs 16:18 MSG

We read about celebrities who act inappropriately, commit crimes, and overdose on drugs. Some spend time in prison for their actions. Perhaps their false sense of pride and security in their fame gave them permission to make wrong choices, never believing they would be held accountable. I imagine some people gloat when the high and mighty are caught with their hands in the cookie jar. There is an old saying, "The bigger they are, the harder they fall."

Let's bring this attitude closer to home, away from slick magazine covers and tabloids. Our addicts operate from inflated pride and continue in their addiction, ruining their own lives and their families' as well. Often they are too proud to ask for help. They think they can wrestle the monkey on their backs without assistance or input. For a time that may be possible, but long-term, sustainable recovery is the result of humbly asking for assistance.

Step One of the Twelve Steps sets the prideful attitude at the back of the line and acknowledges the need for help. "We admitted that we were powerless over our addiction, that our lives had become unmanageable." That one sentence takes the first step toward a new life free from the chains and confines of addiction.

I have a dear friend who is a crack addict. For years I tried to get her help, but she always found excuses not to enter treatment. She told me she could stop; after all, she had been in treatment six times before. Eight years ago I convinced her to give sober living another try. She checked into a faith-based recovery program and graduated. Her sobriety lasted two months. The past eight years have been a living hell watching her waste away with her drug of choice. A year ago, through tears, she said, "Sharron, I need help. I can't do this by myself; it's bigger than I am. Will you take me back to the Center?" She humbly admitted her powerlessness over drugs and went back to the program from which she graduated eight years ago.

Pride keeps addicts sick. Until our sons, daughters, or spouses come to the end of their rope and ask for help, we have to wait. We hurt when they abuse substances and misbehave, but we can be prepared with a plan when they bury their pride and bend the knee to their captor. Now they are ready for Step One.

Extend all the love and grace you can muster during this vulnerable time. Consider what it took for your loved one to say, "Help me. I can't do this alone."

DAILY PRAYER

Dear Lord, I set aside my own pride and offer myself as a vessel of your love, grace, and mercy to my loved one. May I extend help in such a way he will see Jesus through my actions. Amen.

REFLECTION

Do you struggle with pride? Is pride an issue for your addict?

DAY 49: HEALING TEARS

Jesus wept.

John 11:35 NIV

Today's verse is the shortest verse in the Bible, but it communicates volumes about Jesus' love for his friend, Lazarus, who had died. Some in the crowd criticized Jesus for allowing Lazarus' death, missing his broken heart.

If I had a nickel for every tear shed over the last fifteen years, I think I could pay cash for a new car, maybe even a house.

Mothers tend to be more emotional than fathers so our tears come as no big surprise. Some moms cry so much their weeping loses its effectiveness. But when the dad sheds tears it draws attention.

I recall one night when Dan and I had reached the end of our emotional ropes. Josh's behavior baffled and terrified us, and we didn't know what to do or where to look for help. We were lying in bed, holding each other as we both sobbed uncontrollably. I could barely speak. Dan's grief matched mine, tear for tear.

Before going to bed I read the story of Abraham preparing to sacrifice Isaac, his only son, at God's command. As Abraham lifted the knife in obedience, God supplied a substitute sacrifice, a ram caught in a bramble. The message I took from the scripture revolved around Abraham's willingness to place his son on the altar, even unto death.

That night as Dan and I wept together, we placed Josh on God's altar. We told him our son was in his hands, and we took our hands off. I finally said the words no parent dreams of saying, "Father, if it means taking my son's life to heal him of this addiction, then I lay him down and give him fully to you."

The night my husband and I shared tears of sorrow and hope is counted among one of the most special and significant experiences of our marriage. His vulnerable tears spoke of his love for me, our son, and our family.

DAILY PRAYER

Sweet Lord, thank you for the tears mothers and fathers shed for their children. You understand the pain of seeing someone you love suffering and sick. Grant our tears are not shed in vain. May restoration come through their saltiness. Amen.

REFLECTION

Has your loved one seen you cry because of his or her addiction? Describe a time you and your loved one shared tears.

DAY 50: CARING FOR OUR FUTURE

Children's children are a crown to the aged.

Proverbs 17:6a NIV

I love my five grandchildren. They call me Mimi, and my heart flutters each time I hear their sweet voices say the name. My four-year-old grandson, Cayden, pronounces it "Meemee" with his smooth southern drawl. I melt anew when he calls to me. As much as I adore my grandbabies, I pray I never become responsible for their full-time care.

The 2000 U.S. Census reports that over 2.4 million grandparents have responsibility for their grandchildren, a staggering number to digest.

Not all of these children fall under their grandparents' tutelage because of non-caring, wayward parents. The reasons are as varied as the families involved. Sometimes death claims one or both parents. In many cases, parents are incarcerated. Or, mom and dad have substance abuse problems and can no longer properly care for their children. What becomes of these precious ones?

The alternative to family care is state-run agencies, orphanages, or foster care. Horror stories of abuse while in foster homes or orphanages make headlines in newspapers across the country. Bad behaviors and poor choices by parents land their innocent children in settings ripe for mistreatment.

If you find yourself in the position of caring for your

grandchildren, I applaud you for stepping up to the plate when your adult child cannot or will not shoulder his or her responsibilities. I commend you for reaching deep to love that vulnerable child.

Circumstances outside their control burden children beyond their tender years, and overwhelm you in your golden ones. Praying for your grandchild's parents may prove difficult, but they need prayer more than ever before. Ask God to bring someone into their path to encourage and strengthen their resolve to turn their lives around. I pray the children entrusted to your care will feel your love enveloping them like a warm blanket.

Take care of yourself emotionally and spiritually. Hopefully you have a church family to provide encouragement and support.

Jesus holds a special place in his heart for children. To the grandparents selflessly caring for their grandchildren, I think he carries an honored spot for you too.

DAILY PRAYER

Dear Father, bless grandparents tonight with an extra measure of strength and courage as they, for whatever reasons, rear their grandbabies. Wrap your arms around them as they embrace, love and protect their precious ones. Amen.

REFLECTION

Do you have grandchildren? How do you influence your grandbabies to avoid addiction?

DAY 51: HELPER OR ENABLER?

Discipline your son, for in that there is hope; do not be a willing party to his death.

Proverbs 19:18 NIV

I hate admitting I was an enabler. In my mind I was a helper. My intentions and motivations were pure, but I now realize they were destructive and prolonged the agony for Josh and our family.

The definition of an enabler, in its most simple form, is someone who assists another person to continue in self-destructive behaviors, as in substance abuse, by providing resources and excuses or by helping the individual avoid the consequences of his behavior.

I'm guilty on all points.

Josh had a friend I didn't like. Our dachshund, Heidi, didn't like him, either. He should have taken a clue from Heidi to walk away from this young man. When the two got together, trouble clung to them like magnets. I cringed when this friend called or came by our house.

He stopped by one day to get Josh, but he wasn't at home. That left me to entertain him during the wait. Being a polite Southern belle, I stayed in the kitchen and tried to carry on a conversation. I don't remember what I said, but he lashed out at me, cursing and telling me that Josh's problems were my fault. "You @!#% give him whatever he wants. He takes no responsibility for what he does because you @!#% get him out of trouble all the time!"

Dumbfounded that he used such foul language at me, I walked out and left him waiting alone for Josh to come home. I was crushed because he was right. It took a kid I didn't like to speak the truth—certainly not spoken in love. His words got my attention to how my enabling behaviors harmed my son.

The parenting tightrope is fraught with tension. Lean too far to the right, and you'll fall. Sway too far to the left, and you'll smack into the ground. Walking the straight and narrow is difficult. The book of Proverbs is chock full of wisdom for raising our children God's way. Today's verse implies focused effort, including personal sacrifice, dedication, and training with a goal of teaching right living. We have a small window of opportunity to instill positive characteristics in our children.

Take a look at yourself, asking God to illuminate the areas rife with enabling behaviors. Be willing to make the necessary changes so that you can discipline while there is yet hope.

DAILY PRAYER

Dear Lord, guide me tonight as I parent my child. Forgive the times I failed to be a helper and enabled poor choices and behavior. My pure motives often become misdirected. Your divine intervention can happen in my addict's life if I will step out of your way. Amen.

REFLECTION

Are you an enabler for your addict? What can you do differently to help without enabling?

DAY 52: IT ALL COUNTS

You've kept track of my every toss and turn through the sleepless nights. Each tear entered in your ledger, each ache written in your book.

Psalm 58:6 MSG

I write notes in my Bible's margins as I read the scriptures or listen to sermons. I like to reread the notes and reflect on what prompted them. The comments beside today's scripture read, "Are a mother's tears for her children recorded on your scroll? Are my tears forever etched in your record? My tears have been many, but you were faithful through all of them. You turned my weeping into joy."

The disease of addiction brings heavy burdens to parents, spouses, friends, and strangers. I know of at least four families living through horrendous circumstances with their addicted loved ones. One young man has three precious children, a wife, and an opiate addiction. He's also the not-too-proud owner of an orange jumpsuit issued by his local jail. He's facing felony charges that could put him away for many years. Another young man is drinking himself into an early grave, but he's oblivious to the pain he's causing his parents. He says it's his life, and he can do what he wants with it. He's always gotten his way, and sees no reason to stop.

The third, a friend's nephew, overdosed and went into treatment. He walked out of the facility and into the path of an oncoming car, an apparent suicide attempt. Family members are beside themselves with grief. The driver of the car, a total stranger, is now affected by this young man's addiction. The fourth family lost a beautiful daughter to a drug overdose. Friends gathered in the ICU waiting room supporting her mother, grappling with details of the situation.

These families could fill fifty-gallon barrels with their tears. However, encouragement comes from knowing that our heavenly Father keeps track of them. He knows the aching in their hearts. The verse for today says he's keeping a ledger account of the despair. Perhaps the joy he will bring at their recovery will be equal to the tears they've shed. He assures each drop will be balanced with an equal smile and lightness of heart. Now, that will make your heart sing, won't it?

Take courage from your sorrow. Know that your heavenly Father cares and will restore your joy.

DAILY PRAYER

Dear compassionate Lord, thank you for your journal entries each time a tear is shed for a loved one. By faith we look forward to the restoration of joy that addiction has sucked away. Watch over our loved ones and give them back their joy. Amen.

REFLECTION

Could you count the tears shed for your loved one? Describe the ache in your heart.

DAY 53: KEEP IT CLEAN

When a defiling evil spirit is expelled from someone, it drifts along through the desert looking for an oasis, some unsuspecting soul it can bedevil. When it doesn't find anyone, it says, "I'll go back to my old haunt." On return it finds the person spotlessly clean, but vacant.

Matthew 12:43-44 MSG

Spring-cleaning has been around for centuries. Historically, houses remained closed up during brutal winter months. They were heated with wood and coal and by the time the warmth of spring beckoned, soot and ash covered everything in the house. At spring's arrival, the woman of the house flung open the windows and cleaning began in earnest.

The scripture for today uses spring-cleaning as a word picture of what happens in our hearts when we accept Jesus as our Savior. Symbolically, Jesus sweeps away the accumulated soot and ash, leaving the rooms of our hearts spotless. After he sanitizes our lives, we can pass the "white glove" test.

Our addicts must do the same as the cleaning woman. They take the first step by laying down their drug or behavior of choice. Then what? They attend one or two meetings a week and then quit going. An excuse to skip a meeting always pops up. Former, unsafe friends reappear and they start hanging out like they did in the past. Items go missing; then cash vanishes from your wallet. Before you know it, your addict is in full relapse, and the cycle begins anew.

While stopping the drugs or alcohol is important, it is more important that new, positive behaviors replace the old. The recommendation to attend ninety meetings in ninety days is to instill new patterns of behavior and to find new acquaintances who share a common desire for sobriety.

Complacency breeds relapse. Matthew 12:45 says that the evil spirit returns to the clean house, taking seven more spirits with him, and the final condition of the man is worse than the first. Relapse can be worse, and more dangerous, than the previous active addiction state. Depending on how long your loved ones were clean and sober, returning to using can be especially difficult for their bodies to handle and an overdose can occur.

The challenge for family members is to encourage their addict's continued commitment to recovery. With proper boundaries in place, cheer on their day-to-day victories over the monkey on their back. Help them visualize life apart from addiction.

Spring-cleaning is never done; the season rolls around every year. Dust accumulates and must be wiped away regularly. The same applies for sobriety. The job of working the Twelve Steps is never over. It is the "one day at a time" tidying that keeps dust bunnies at bay.

DAILY PRAYER

Lord of spring-cleaning, thank you for washing my heart and ridding it of dirt and grime. May the sparkle of your cleansing touch wash over my loved one tonight. Remove the cobwebs from his mind to reveal the clarity of your will for his life. Amen.

REFLECTION

Do you perform spring-cleaning? Write down your spring-cleaning ritual.

DAY 54: HITTING BOTTOM

When he came to his senses .... he got up and went to his father.

Luke 15: 17, 20 NIV

The parable of the prodigal son rings familiar to many people. The verses in Luke 15: 11-31 provide much fodder for sermons, books, and magazine articles. Why does this years-old story still resonate with us in the twenty-first century?

Perhaps you view your addicted loved one as a prodigal, the child or spouse who chose a different path that ultimately led to destruction. You can relate to the father in the Bible story as he waits patiently for his son to return home from living a life of debauchery in a foreign country. You, too, wait patiently for your loved one to turn his or her back on a negative way of life.

The young man in the parable squandered his inheritance on parties, women, and wild living. When the money ran out, so did his friends. His partying and indulgences desensitized him to his upbringing and core beliefs. He found himself, a Jewish man, feeding pigs and eating pig slop. In Jewish culture, pigs were considered unclean and could not be touched or eaten. The young man was in a desperate place emotionally, spiritually, and financially.

The scripture says when he came to his senses he realized his father's slaves had more than he did. After realizing the slaves had food, clothing, and shelter, he decided to go back home. He would offer himself as a servant to his father even though he was the landowner's son.

In Twelve Step verbiage, the realization of addiction's consequences is called "hitting bottom" and it is different for each person. The bottom may involve an overdose, an arrest, or a stint in jail or prison. For others the bottom is a divorce or bankruptcy. For my son, the insight came when he recognized the activities in which he was involved jeopardized a future with his son and wife. At that point, the desire to be a loving, present father and husband was stronger than the lure of drugs. He pulled himself from the pit he was in and began the journey to a new life.

What about your addicted loved one? Has he or she hit bottom yet? Are you prepared emotionally and spiritually when that day comes? In the story of the prodigal son, the father expectantly watched and waited for his son. Filled with compassion, he welcomed him home and threw a big party in his honor; his boy was back.

Choosing to leave the pigsty of addiction takes courage and humility. When you see your loved one approaching, remember the example set by this father and welcome your wanderer home.

DAILY PRAYER

Dear Father, God of second chances, thank you for waiting for me with open arms. Thank you that my arms were open to receive my loved one when he reached the bottom of his pit. Bless families struggling with a wandering child or spouse with patience, compassion, and courage as they patiently wait for their loved one to come back home. Amen.

REFLECTION

Recount a time when you came to your senses regarding your loved one. What action did you take to bring about change?

DAY 55: UNACCEPTABLE RISK

> *You're addicted to thrills? What an empty life! The pursuit of pleasure is never satisfied.*
>
> **Proverbs 21:17 MSG**

I'm not a risk taker. I appreciate and need the security of staying within the straight lines. Gambling doesn't interest me because I know I risk losing my money if I don't play my cards right or bet on the losing team.

Some people love the thrill and excitement of taking risks. Divers who jump off cliffs wearing flying parachute pants baffle me. As I watch them hurl themselves from mountaintops, I rehearse every possible scenario that could contribute to their deaths. I don't enjoy watching their stunts as I anticipate a messy ending.

My teenagers took unnecessary risks that they considered no big deal like skipping school and underage drinking. My oldest daughter tried parachuting and loved it. Our family experienced the thrill with her as we watched the video. Her excited screams testified to the fun she was having as she plummeted toward the ground. On the other hand, I would never voluntarily jump from an airplane unless it was on fire.

As a toddler, our son had no fear. He would jump off anything, eat anything (except sour cream) or drink anything. He picked up bugs, lizards and other critters and teased his sisters with them.

During his preteen and teen years, his thrill seeking took a dark turn—drugs and alcohol. Bugs and lizards no longer held the same fascination. Each level of usage and experimentation increased the constant need for more and more. His partying lifestyle and being the go-to-guy for drugs and alcohol became as much of an addiction as the substances.

Today's scripture sounds a warning to adrenaline addicts: Your pursuit of pleasure is never satisfied. Each attempt to feed the craving ratchets up the risk of injury, arrest, and possibly, death. These activities may create financial burdens on the family much like substance addiction.

The challenge for parents or spouses of these thrill seekers is to help them realize the emptiness of their pursuits. We want to encourage athletic prowess and having fun, but we also need to point out the dangers and the futility of chasing something that can't be caught. There is always one more thrill over the next mountain or beyond the next giant, rolling wave.

Because moderation balances successful thrill-seeking behaviors, encourage your loved one to practice moderation every day.

DAILY PRAYER

Dear Father, thank you for my loved one. I thank you he loves to have fun. I'm grateful he brings joy and excitement to a sometime dull world. Help him to understand and desire moderation in all things. May he seek to temper risk-taking behaviors. Watch over and protect him this day. Amen.

REFLECTION

Are you a risk taker? What attracts you to adrenaline-boosting activities? Does that help you understand your addict's risk-taking behaviors?

DAY 56: WHAT IF?

Do your best, prepare for the worst—then trust God to bring victory.

Proverbs 21:31 MSG

Today's verse smacks of contrasts. We are admonished to do our best, but be prepared for the worst. I almost want to say, "Why bother?" If something bad occurs in spite of my best efforts, I don't feel motivated to excel.

I tried to be the best mom I could be. As a family, we regularly attended church and taught our children about God and Jesus. I cooked, cleaned, and chauffeured kids to dance lessons and ball practice, but nothing I did kept *the worst* from invading our family. What more could I have done?

My best parenting occurred when the children were younger. Our lives were less complicated and pressures appeared lighter. Of course, we had parenting challenges, but none that rose to the level of those experienced in their teen years. The seeds of faith took root during their early years even though the fruit was scant in the rebellious ones.

I'm not sure how a parent prepares for the worst. I didn't have a crystal ball to reveal the shape *worst* would take. The local community college didn't offer a class in "Disaster Training for Parents," although it sounds like a good idea.

Hindsight allowed me to see that my spiritual foundation from childhood carried me through the rough periods. I drew strength from verses I memorized as a child. I recalled the lyrics of hymns and my faith remained steady. The faith-filled examples of my parents and grandparents demonstrated how to rise above life's calamities.

The verse today says to "do your best, prepare for the worst" and trust God with the victory. Our part of the equation is to arm ourselves spiritually. A solid foundation puts us in a position to step aside and trust God with the outcome. That belief in God builds upon itself with each victory.

Are you prepared for your worst-case scenario? We don't like to think about those tough situations—arrest, overdose, or death—because they are unpleasant. Formulate some "what if" questions, preparing for the eventuality of the worst. Don't obsess on these scenarios, but consider the possibilities. Create an action plan ... just in case that "what if" becomes your here and now reality.

God will guide and comfort you during these times as you seek him, believing in faith he holds the key to your loved one's successful recovery.

DAILY PRAYER

Dear Victorious Father, thank you for the battles you have fought for my family. Help my faith to grow through preparation, trusting you with the outcome. Thank you for the victory we have through Jesus. Amen.

REFLECTION

How do you prepare yourself for bad news? Do you trust God to bring victory to your addict?

DAY 57: ROCK SOLID

Rain poured down, the river flooded, a tornado hit—but nothing moved that house. It was fixed to the rock.

Matthew 7:25 MSG

Today's verse paints a beautiful word picture of an addict's family. In the story Jesus told, a man built a house, perhaps his dream home, on a base of solid rock. One day a storm blew in, bringing torrential rains and winds. I envision a hurricane or tornado wreaking havoc on the man's handiwork. The storm pounded the house with great ferocity, but it remained standing because of its foundation.

My husband and I have solid spiritual foundations. Our parents took us to church from infancy and instilled godly principles. They encouraged us to continue in our faith walks and, by example, showed us how to do it. They prepared us spiritually for storms that lay ahead.

When our children reached their teen years, our foundations took a pounding. The category five hurricane-force winds of rebellion and disobedience battered us, but we remained fixed on God's promises of provision and protection for our family.

The story in Matthew 7 continues by comparing the solid rock builder to a man who built his house on sand. Another storm came and battered his home. Fierce winds swirled and rain drenched the ground. The house collapsed because it was built on sand. Just as sand shifts, rock remains.

Families of addicts are desperate for something to cling to when the storms of addiction assault their loved ones. Friends and family members often provide an anchor during the tempests, but a deep abiding faith in God outlasts those relationships. Friends grow weary of our tales of woe and crises, but God doesn't. He is the rock on which our security rests.

Interestingly, sand is rock that has been ground up or beaten into small particles. Do you feel you've been pulverized because of addiction? I do. Some days I felt no bigger than a grain of sand, worn down by circumstances beyond my control. It seemed my house was collapsing around me.

God assured me his word was true and that my belief was solid. The night I read Jeremiah 30 and 31, he gathered my sand-like particles of disbelief, hurt, and worry and restored them to a rock of hope and faith.

DAILY PRAYER

Holy Rock, my Father, thank you for reforming and restoring the specks of my disbelief into a rock of faith. Thank you for allowing the storms to show your greatness and provision. Amen.

REFLECTION

What is your life's foundation built upon? How unshakable is it?

DAY 58: SHOW ME

Your cleansed and grateful life, not your words, will bear witness to what I have done.

Matthew 8:4b MSG

Jesus healed more than one leper. We often hear about the ten lepers in Luke 17 who stopped Jesus as he walked between Samaria and Galilee. All ten were healed, but only one returned to express thankfulness.

The diseased man in today's passage was alone. He saw Jesus and knelt before him and said, "Master, if you want to, you can heal my body." Jesus reached out and touched him saying, "I want to. Be clean."

The custom of the day required the man to present himself to the priest who would declare him clean. Jesus instructed this leper to keep the healing quiet and go to the priest as the law of Moses commanded. The man's life would bear witness, not his words, of the miracle Jesus performed.

It is easy to talk about deliverance and healings, but another to live our lives delivered and healed. When our addicts proclaim they have quit using, we often doubt their words based on experience. Too many times we have been stung by another relapse or arrest, so their words ring empty.

One of the chief benefits of the Twelve Steps program revolves around accountability. Sharing in a meeting about sobriety is one thing; living sober is quite another. That message is what Jesus gave to the leper: Don't talk about your healing, live it.

For the addicts in our lives, living clean and sober is the evidence we need to prove their words are not hollow. When they work the Twelve Steps and commit to recovery, one day at a time, our confidence is bolstered that their commitment to sobriety is the real deal. How many times have we heard the following? "I swear things will be different this time. I will never drink again. I promise you, it's over!"

Our family heard variations of those promises from Josh through the years. When he said them, he believed they were true, but nothing in his life changed. People, places, and things tied to drugs and alcohol continued to influence his decisions and behaviors. Mere words could not cut the cords. He had to put feet to his promises. On February 18, 2010 he did.

An old saying, "the proof is in the pudding," sums up recovery for me. Don't talk about changing your life or not using drugs again—show me, one day at a time.

DAILY PRAYER

Dear Lord, thank you for your willingness to heal and make whole those broken places in our lives. Bless my loved one tonight as he puts actions to his promises. Amen.

REFLECTION

Is it easier to tell people about the antics of your addict or to share what God has done in your life in spite of his or her misbehavior?

DAY 59: DEALING WITH FAMILY PATTERNS

Don't be like your parents.

Zechariah 1:4a MSG

A friend and I were shopping in a department store. I tried on an outfit and stepped in front of a wall of mirrors to check myself and to get my friend's comments. As I looked into the mirror, I said, "Oh my word! It's Tish." The salesperson looked around for "Tish," but there was no one there but my friend and me.

"Who's Tish?" she asked.

"My mother," I said. "I've become my mother. She has a camel and black striped shirt just like this one. I look like my mother!" It seems each passing year I resemble her more and more.

God's first message to the young prophet Zechariah required he tell the children of Israel not to be like their parents. Their parents and grandparents were disobedient and ultimately it cost them their lives. The warning was a reminder to make better decisions or the same end would come to their generation.

In the heat of an argument or chaotic situation, a parent hurls the invective, "You are just like your mother!" or "You're a no-good loser, just like your father!" If that assessment is accurate, the teen or adult, will not sense a need to be anything different. Constant reminders of worthlessness plant deep roots difficult to pull out.

Too often, addicts use these emotional criticisms as an excuse to continue using and for other misbehaviors. "If I'm just like my dad, what's the use in trying to be anything different?" It's the "apple doesn't fall far from the tree" mentality.

Today's verse admonishes us not to repeat the poor choices of our parents and grandparents. We can't deny physical likenesses and even mannerisms, but we can refuse to follow in their unacceptable habits and behaviors. Just because a parent was an addict doesn't mean the child will become an addict. One's parentage may create difficulties, but it is not a slam dunk to skid row or prison.

With love and grace, help your children recognize family behavior patterns and steer them in another direction. Name-calling and belittling will do little to create life change. Acknowledge their deficiencies and choose to encourage new behavior.

DAILY PRAYER

Lord, thank you for godly parents. Help me set a good example of right living for my children. Bless my children with courage and wisdom not to repeat dysfunctional family patterns. Amen.

REFLECTION

Have you ever spewed, "You're just like your father (or mother)" at your addict? Did it change his or her behavior?

DAY 60: CAPTIVE TO DECEPTION

Then you will know the truth, and the truth will set you free.

John 8:32 NIV

The world watched in horror as Iranian students took fifty-two American hostages by storming the U.S. Embassy in Tehran on November 4, 1979. The Americans' contact with their families and friends was cut off. Diplomatic efforts failed to procure their release. A failed military extrication and economic sanctions against Iran proved fruitless as well. The death of Egypt's shah and the invasion of Iran by Iraq broke the logjam of negotiations.

Because of addiction, many families find themselves in strikingly similar situations as the hostage taking in Iran. We are going about our day-to-day routines when, all of a sudden, the normalcy of our lives is jerked away by unrelenting enemies—drugs, alcohol, or gambling. The addicts in our lives impose economic sanctions on us by borrowing or stealing money and possessions. Relationships with friends and family members are cut off because of embarrassment or fear.

Notice it took a death and invasion of a country's personal space before change occurred. The same thing happens in our families. It is often the death of a loved one that awakens us to the adversary invading our lives and families. Until tragedy strikes, interest in the addiction culture takes a backseat to more acceptable lifestyles. We're held captive to its deception until the truth of our loved one's situation is acknowledged.

Can you imagine the American hostages volunteering to be captured again and held against their will? Imagine their captors telling them conditions will be better if they return. They might even enjoy it!

That scenario stretches our imaginations, yet recapture happens all the time in families struggling with an addict. Periods of sobriety are blown to smithereens by relapse. Once again, addicts and their families are taken hostage by an unforgiving, misleading foe.

Today's verse says that by knowing the truth we will be set free. It doesn't imply physical freedom, although that can occur. I think Jesus intimated spiritual and emotional freedom of the prisons in our souls and spirits. Truth sometimes brings pain, but the discomfort prods us to look for help, to make changes in attitudes and lifestyles, and to become the individuals and families God intended.

Seek truth before tragedy strikes.

DAILY PRAYER

Dear Lord, reveal the truth of your goodness to me tonight. Show me the areas where I am held captive. I thank you for the liberty I have in knowing you. I pray that my loved one will also walk in your truth. Amen.

REFLECTION

Explain what freedom looks like for you and your family.

DAY 61: BEHIND CLOSED DOORS

Better to live alone in a tumbledown shack than share a mansion with a nagging spouse.

Proverbs 25:24 MSG

I'm thankful I didn't grow up in a household marked by screaming, yelling, and objects being lobbed at me or a wall. Our children didn't witness that kind of behavior, either.

Many homes, however, are private battlegrounds hidden behind closed doors and curtained windows. I only know from being told about fathers coming home drunk and beating their wife, girlfriend, or children. Some people are "mean drunks" and lash out with words and fists. Others are subdued. They retreat to a quiet corner to pass out or watch the world swirl by.

Fighting + bickering = nagging. Does the size of your bank account determine if you'll become a nag? Of course not. Our verse today implies that the wealthy can be miserable right along with the middle and lower classes. A fat checkbook doesn't guarantee happiness any more than being poor ensures a life of misery.

The addict may end up with less floor space, but at least the nagging stopped and recovery became the focus, not persistent harassment.

Have you considered what constant nagging, screaming, and fighting does to your addict and to other family members? Although much of the nagging comes from frustration, anger, and disappointment, in the greater scheme of resolution and restoration it accomplishes little. Self-esteem continues to plummet, relationships churn in a sea of unrest and flux and, in the end, someone leaves the home.

The verse for today speaks of a mansion; this can be figurative as well as literal since most families don't live in mansions.

Nagging fails to nurture positive changes. It undermines recovery and creates additional tension. I recommend *Get Your Loved One Sober: Alternatives to Nagging, Pleading, and Threatening* by Robert J. Myers and Brenda L. Wolfe. Drs. Myers and Wolfe outline behavior modifications to relieve the stress and tensions brought on by addictions. Dr. Myers grew up in an alcoholic home, and he understands well the dynamics of an alcoholic family.

As part of your daily journal time, review the previous day's conversations, looking for nagging, contentious traits and commit to make some changes. The difference in your home will be amazing.

DAILY PRAYER

Dear Lord, forgive me when I nag and gripe at my addict. Help me to see him through your eyes and accept him right where he is. Encourage growth by boundaries and a gentle spirit. Amen.

REFLECTION

Write your thoughts about today's verse. Would you consider living alone if it brought peace?

DAY 62: THAT'S CRAZY!

As a dog returns to its vomit, so a fool repeats his folly.

Proverbs 26:11 NIV

The standard AA and NA definition for insanity is doing the same thing over and over expecting a different outcome.

A dog returning to eat its own vomit is a graphic example of insanity. The mental image is revolting. I've seen dogs do it and almost hurled while watching. The obvious question is, "Why would an animal do that?" When I Googled "Why do dogs eat their vomit?" I found I'm not the only one asking the question. There is no definitive answer for this disgusting behavior. They just do it.

But we're not dogs. Humans have the capability to think, reason, and formulate responses to stimuli. Animals don't have the capacity to experience the highs and lows of emotions like humans. Since we differ from Fido, why do we imitate this nauseating behavior? It doesn't make sense, but that's the insanity of our species.

Addiction makes no sense to a non-addict. A friend, fresh out of rehab, and I discussed a mutual friend who holds the traditional "just quit" view of recovery. Don't use drugs. End of discussion. Our friend doesn't understand the lure of the drug and why someone would go back to it.

The scripture for today speaks of relapse in the context of our lives as family members of an addict. What can we do to encourage our loved one to walk away from the retch of addiction? Each family will have to tailor appropriate corrective actions to their situations. But, we can first look within ourselves for attitudes or behaviors the addict gives as an excuse for using. Remember yesterday's verse on nagging and contentiousness? Addicts use drowning out incessant yakking as an excuse to get high or drunk.

While we criticize their relapses, we also return to our own vomit when we continue condemning, fighting, and enabling, expecting a different result. Professional addiction counselors can assist family members in gauging the situation and formulating a plan to refrain from the foolish patterns of harmful behaviors.

Break insanity's hold on your family. Try a different approach and see what happens.

DAILY PRAYER

Dear Father, thank you for lessons learned from our four-legged friends. Help me recognize when I'm returning to destructive actions that tear down rather than build up. My addict needs help here too. I pray the lure of recovery is stronger than the scent of vomit. Amen.

REFLECTION

What is your definition of insanity? Relate the definition to your family.

DAY 63:
THAT DAY-AT-A-TIME THING

Don't brashly announce what you're going to do tomorrow; you don't know the first thing about tomorrow.

Proverbs 27:1 MSG

Abraham Lincoln said, "The best thing about the future is that it comes one day at a time." That's strikingly similar to "one day at a time," the Twelve Step mantra that reminds our addicts to work on their recovery for a twenty-four hour period at a time. Family members who live by organizers and smartphones find this kind of narrowed living challenging.

Of course, we have to plan our work weeks, school activities, and other events, but we execute our plans on a daily basis. We can't cram five years of living into twenty-four hours. In Matthew 6:34 (MSG), Jesus said, "Give your attention to what God is doing right now, and don't get worked up about what may or may not happen tomorrow. God will help you deal with whatever hard things come up when the time comes." Planning not only alleviates worry but also it allows room for God's guidance.

Too often family members heap unrealistic schedules on their newly recovering addict. They stand poised to pass out milestone chips (AA) and key rings (NA) to addicts fresh out of rehab. I was guilty of planning my son's future clean time while he was in treatment. During our telephone conversations, I would say, "Just think, when you've got five years clean ..." After a while, Josh corrected me with this statement, "Mom, time takes time. I can't think about five years from now."

Time does take time—minute by minute, hour by hour. Days turn into weeks. Weeks roll into months, and months become years, but each was added one day at a time. As family members, we are excited and expectant that our loved one is clean and sober, and we want to see the long-term markers of right living. A ten-year sobriety key ring sounds wonderful after years of living with an addict. Projecting future sobriety beyond *today* is placing unnecessary stress on our addicts. Allow them to do the "next right thing" today and tomorrow will take care of itself.

Abraham Lincoln never attended a Twelve Step meeting, but he certainly hit the mark with his comment, "The best thing about the future is that it comes one day at a time."

DAILY PRAYER

Dear Father of days, thank you for giving me today to love you and serve you. Help me to understand fully one day at a time so I don't pressure my loved one about his future. Guide his steps as he chooses to live his twenty-four hours doing the next right thing. Thank you for the Twelve Steps and for the life change they have brought to countless families. Amen.

REFLECTION

Explain how you view planning. Are you a structured, detailed planner? Or do you live your life haphazardly, by the seat of your pants?

DAY 64: SPRINGING THE TRAP

Have I now become your enemy by telling you the truth?
Galatians 4:16

Pastor David Fairchild told the following story in a sermon on freedom and release from the pain of poor choices:

"This is the story of a bear whose foot is caught in a trap. A man sees the trapped bear and approaches it. He loads his gun and shoots. After being shot, the bear begins to swing wildly at the man, and just as the bear loses consciousness, the man steps closer. The bear feels the man taking his paw, pushing it deeper into the trap causing more pain.

"What do you think the bear was thinking just before he passed out? *This guy loves me, he's here to save me and take care of me.*

"No, the bear was thinking that he was trapped and shot by this man. The last thing the bear feels is the pain of his paw being pushed deeper into the trap. The bear doesn't know the shooter is a park ranger using a tranquilizer gun. The ranger pushed the bear's foot deeper into the trap in order to release its hold on the paw. The release mechanism lay beneath the bear's foot. The wounded paw received care once it was freed from the trap."

This story portrays addiction. Our addicts are ensnared by their drug or behavior of choice and struggle to free themselves from its powerful clutches. We family members represent the park ranger doing what is necessary to free our loved one, often a pain-inflicting process. We make tough choices that our addicts perceive as more injury. We may put them out of the house or cut them off financially until healing takes place. We do what is necessary to save their lives and our own.

Their lives are at risk, just like the bear's. They will experience physical, emotional, and spiritual discomfort as they seek release from their traps. The support of Twelve Step groups, medical or counseling professionals, and family members provide ways out of the deadly deception called addiction.

In today's verse Paul asked the Galatians, "Have I become your enemy by telling you the truth?" Of course he wasn't their enemy. His love for the people of Galatia compelled him to speak the truth in love.

As difficult as it is, speak the truth *in love* to your addict. Do what is necessary to release the trap and allow the healing to begin.

DAILY PRAYER

Dear Lord, may my addict's life intersect with someone who cares enough to spring the trap of addiction and make a way to freedom. Where there is pain, provide comfort. Let freedom begin with me. Amen.

REFLECTION

Truth is often painful. Recall a time when hearing the truth caused you pain.

DAY 65: LESS-THAN

When the woman saw that the fruit of the tree was good for food and pleasing to the eye, and also desirable for gaining wisdom, she took some and ate it.

Genesis 3:6a NIV

The story of Adam and Eve in the Garden of Eden is familiar to most people. The plight of the world rests on their shoulders because of their disobedience. God cursed Eve's childbearing with pain, and, for those women who have borne children we know the curse is real. Adam's curse involved labor and work. God told him he would sweat and work hard to eke out an existence. Providing for his family would be difficult. These themes are common to us.

I attended a women's Bible study and a new perspective for these scriptures was introduced: inadequacy. The study leader said when she read the familiar passage in Genesis 3 the word *inadequacy* kept popping into her mind. Her comments resonated in my spirit as I turned the word over and over in my own mind.

Eve and her husband had everything, their lives were perfect, but a beguiling creature suggested to Eve that she didn't possess everything. The serpent proposed that she was not as wise as God. She lacked something and, because of her lack, she was inadequate.

Most of us have more possessions and pedigrees than we need: cars, houses, boats, education. Yet we feel inadequate because we don't have *it* all. These feelings get us in trouble when we make choices trying to bolster our self-image and self-worth.

Consuming the most alcohol at a party is sometimes an attempt to achieve recognition, to stand out in the crowd. A young woman thinks her body is flawed; in her mind she is undesirable. Acting out sexually squelches her *less-than* thoughts, at least for a short time. A spouse going into debt to purchase the latest trendy gadget boosts his or her ego until the next new one hits the market. These examples show how easily our loved ones fall into the trap of believing the *you are not enough* lie.

Pay attention to your loved one and note signs of inadequacy. Your son, daughter, or spouse might say, "I never do anything right." Or, "I'm so stupid, nobody likes me." Or, "I'll never find a high-paying job." If your loved one constantly makes self-disparaging comments, watch for changes in attitude, appearance, or friends—a few of the usual warning signs of substance abuse or risky behaviors.

Encourage your loved one and help her understand her worth and importance to your family.

DAILY PRAYER

Dear Lord, thank you that my significance is found in and through your Son, Jesus. Forgive me when I focus on my inadequacies. Let me be an example to my loved one by showing appreciation for her and her uniqueness. Amen.

REFLECTION

Recall your feelings of inadequacy as a wife, husband, father, mother, employee, or friend. How did you overcome the feelings?

DAY 66: THE MOM FACTOR

The rod of correction imparts wisdom, but a child left to himself disgraces his mother.

Proverbs 29:15 NIV

My mother was a stay-at-home mom to four children. She cooked daily meals, mowed the yard, chauffeured us to our after-school activities, and completed a long list of other tasks that kept our house in good working order. When we got home after school, she was there.

Similar scenarios played out each day in the community where I grew up. Most of my friends' mothers did what my mother did—took care of their children and didn't work outside the home. I didn't know any latchkey children.

I began working when our youngest daughter started first grade. Our household was different from the one of my youth. The kinds of tasks my mother completed during the day while we were at school I tackled when I got home in the afternoons.

When we moved to Florida, I found a job and continued working outside our home. The time the kids were alone after school until I got home from work became a breeding ground for trouble when they entered junior high and high schools.

The unsupervised two or three hours provided time for mischief. On several occasions I came home to find tobacco littering our pool deck. I later learned the kids were smoking blunts. A blunt is a cigar that is split open, the tobacco cleaned out and refilled with marijuana, and sometimes laced with other drugs. I was naïve to what was happening in my home. Missing rolls of aluminum foiled had been fashioned into pipes for smoking weed. My inexperience with drugs permitted activities to take place that otherwise would not have been tolerated. I didn't know what I didn't know.

If I had a second chance at parenting, I would have worked part time as my children got older. My presence in the afternoons most likely would have been a deterrent. I like to think it would have made a difference in the eventual outcome, although I'll never know.

Working outside the home and juggling multiple responsibilities can result in unplanned situations. But take courage, your family will survive.

DAILY PRAYER

Sweet Lord, help me to use my time wisely and to spend quality time with my children. May my presence assure them of my love and concern. Amen.

REFLECTION

Working outside the home is an emotional see-saw for moms. If you're a working mom, write how you felt about going back to work after your child's birth.

DAY 67: REACH OUT FOR HELP

But soon word was going around in Judah, "The builders are pooped, the rubbish piles up. We're in over our heads, we can't build this wall."

Nehemiah 4:10 MSG

Nehemiah was the cupbearer for the mighty king Artaxerxes of Susa where the Israelites had lived in exile for decades.

Jerusalem was Nehemiah's spiritual home, but he had never physically seen it. One of his brothers came to visit and Nehemiah asked about Jerusalem. The brother told him the gates were in ruins and the city ripe for attack by their enemies. Nehemiah was distraught at the news.

He asked the king for permission to go to Jerusalem and help rebuild the walls and infrastructure. King Artaxerxes granted the request.

The verses for today tell us that the workers were worn out. They worked hard repairing Jerusalem's walls under brutal, discouraging circumstances. Rubbish and refuse lay scattered in piles. At one point, they threw up their hands and cried, "We're in over our heads."

Sound familiar? As family members to an addict, we know the feelings of exhaustion and despair. At times we feel the emotions are glued to our backs with Super Glue. The refuse and garbage representing our lives lay on the floors of our hearts and homes. On occasion, the crud of our lives ends up splattered in newspaper headlines for the world to see our failures as either parents or spouses. It would be easy to sit in a corner with a blanket over our heads crying, "I can't do this anymore. I've had enough."

Nehemiah didn't allow his countrymen to become discouraged. He took action and developed a plan that would lift them from their despair. He didn't wait for a committee meeting or task force to frame an action list. He didn't blame the government.

He saw a job in need of a leader and stepped up to the plate. Jerusalem's walls were repaired.

Pray God brings a "Nehemiah" into your family's life to encourage you through the tough times, to help formulate an action plan, and to lead you to wholeness.

DAILY PRAYER

Father of plans, guide me to someone who will assess our situation and encourage us through your Word. Direct me to a leader for my loved one who will develop a plan of action leading to wholeness. Help us rebuild the walls of our family. Amen.

REFLECTION

Fatigue frequently drains families burdened with addiction issues. Write down some of your "tired moments" and what you did to rejuvenate yourself.

DAY 68: LOCK THE BACK DOOR

And all this time our enemies were saying, "They won't know what hit them. Before they know it we'll be at their throats, killing them right and left. That will put a stop to the work!"

Nehemiah 4:11 MSG

Night hangs like a black curtain. The stars conceal their twinkling. The intruder slinks along the house as he makes his way to the unlocked back door. Soundlessly, he creeps down the hallway. The family wakes to find themselves captives to an intruder. How did this happen?

Each family member assumed someone else checked the little-used back door, but no one did. No one took responsibility for that first line of defense to keep strangers out. A simple routine left undone resulted in mayhem.

This scenario is fictional, but realistic. Robbers do gain access to homes and businesses through unlocked doors or open windows. They watch for opportunities to enter uninvited. In a similar way, dark forces wage war against families. How have we left our back doors open?

The children of Israel in today's scripture complained of being too busy and exhausted from working on the repairing of the wall. While they complained, their enemies plotted to kill them, swiftly and by surprise. Nehemiah caught wind of the plot and developed a plan to protect the people.

The marathons of hectic schedules leave the back doors of the family's heart vulnerable to attack. Our frantic, overcommitted calendars sap our energy for matters of the heart. Be careful that busyness doesn't choke the planting and nurturing of seeds of faith.

We also open doors by lax attitudes toward movies, music, and videos. We slowly chip away at our family's values by daily incorporating what society approves. How much of our culture's permissiveness is okay?

Nehemiah's strategy included arming each adult with weapons: swords, lances, and bows. Half the workers stood guard while the other half worked. Common laborers held a tool in one hand and a sword in the other. They were were prepared for battle at all times.

Families need a plan of action, a strategy. We should arm ourselves with the weapons of information concerning the intruder, resources to resist should it storm our homes, and the courage to fight. We need to make sure we keep the back door locked, barring enemy access.

Will you be the Nehemiah in your home who will plan the defense, gather the family, and stand against the enemy?

DAILY PRAYER

Dear Father, thank you for protecting my family when enemies pound at our door. I ask for courage to take a stand within my family as I seek to rebuild the holes in our walls. Amen.

REFLECTION

The enemy uses stealth tactics. Write down an incident when the enemy of addiction snuck up on you and your family.

DAY 69: AREAS OF VULNERABILITY

So I stationed armed guards at the most vulnerable places of the wall and assigned people by families with their swords, lances and bows.

Nehemiah 4:13 MSG

The Jews found out about the plot to kill them and started screaming, "They have us surrounded; they're going to attack!" (Neh. 4:12 MSG). Nehemiah had enough of their bellyaching and complaining, so he developed a battle plan.

He stationed armed guards at the most vulnerable places of the wall and assigned the workers in groups by families. They were provided with swords, lances, and bows. He encouraged them to be brave, to remember God Almighty was on their side, and to fight for their brothers, sisters, sons, and daughters, and their homes.

The families were stationed at the portion of the wall outside their homes. The instruction was to fix the broken wall directly in front of their homes. He wanted the home places to be safe and secure for the Jews. He incorporated the deep love of home and family to prompt the best defensive work from the people.

Not only was Nehemiah a phenomenal strategist, but he was also a great source of encouragement for the people of Jerusalem to be and do their very best.

How different do you think our families would be if we armed ourselves, not with weapons, but with knowledge about outside forces targeting family values and ethics that promote hard work?

Our problems won't vanish like fog in the morning sun, but I imagine they would diminish under the togetherness and unity of the family. Are we willing to do our best work with our families?

Are you ready to give it a try? Turn off the TV and computer and spend time with your children. It's never too late to restore relationships. Ask God for wisdom in approaching estranged family members and start the task of rebuilding your family's walls.

Spend time with your child or spouse by participating in their activities. Listen to their music and talk about the lyrics with them. Become aware of their interests and hobbies and ask why they are drawn to a particular area.

If your spouse is the addict, the same strategies can be used. Observe activities he or she enjoys and ask to participate. Build on together time to strengthen your relationship.

The wall of Jerusalem evidenced the touch of families working together to repair the breaches in their defenses. It is my prayer that we will work with the same fervor to mend our broken families.

DAILY PRAYER

Dear Father, I ask for wisdom tonight to guide my family to a place of wholeness where there has been brokenness. Show me the weak places in our family's defenses so we can strengthen them against a formidable enemy. Bless my family this night and keep them safe. Amen.

REFLECTION

Describe a time when you fought for your family's safety and honor.

DAY 70: DON'T GO IT ALONE

God said, "It is not good for the Man to be alone; I'll make him a helper, a companion."

Genesis 2:18 MSG

Y.A.N.A. is a common acronym in recovery rooms. It stands for You Are Not Alone. Simple by design, but powerful in function. In our city there is a Narcotics Anonymous group called Y.A.N.A. The name alone helps dispel the isolation many addicts feel. They often find themselves excluded from family circles because of their addiction. Holidays aren't spent alone but with friends, sometimes strangers, in the recovery rooms. Thankfully Twelve Step groups gather for seasonal celebrations to provide companionship during these vulnerable times.

Our family went to a Fourth of July picnic at an Alcoholic Anonymous meeting house with our son. I was encouraged to see many families there to celebrate but it seemed a bit odd because it wasn't a traditional family gathering. For the men and women at the event, though, it did represent a family gathering borne in the common bond of recovery.

God intended for people to have families and companionship. Today's verse is often quoted at weddings, but its meaning goes beyond a wedding dress, tuxedo, and bridal bouquet. These words reach beyond Adam to include all generations. God created us for fellowship and intimacy, with him and with each other.

Families often isolate themselves because of their loved ones' addictions. The humiliation and embarrassment we feel keeps us behind locked doors and shuttered windows. We don't want anyone to know the truth, even our extended family members. We hold our secrets close.

We dig pits of pity deeper and deeper until we can barely crawl out. We need fellowship and companionship to make it through the tough times. I don't know what I would have done without my husband during the struggles with our son. Many couples' marriages don't survive an addicted spouse or child, but my husband and I grew closer as we united to stand against something determined to destroy our family.

If you find yourself alone in the addiction nightmare, find a support group (Al-Anon, Nar-Anon) or another type fellowship to walk with you in the rough spots. Talk with your pastor, priest, or rabbi and seek godly counsel.

Remember, Y.A.N.A.

DAILY PRAYER

Dear Father, thank you for creating helpers for the alone times. Strengthen me when I feel alone and encourage me to reach out to others who are lonely. Amen.

REFLECTION

Describe a time you felt all alone. What did you do to overcome the feelings?

DAY 71: NOT YOURS TO FIX

Christ has set you free to live a free life. So take your stand! Never again let anyone put a harness of slavery on you.
Galatians 5:1 MSG

On September 8, 2000, my son entered a drug treatment program at a homeless shelter. His dad and I had reached the end of the proverbial rope and put him out of our home two days earlier. The shelter became a safe haven from the storm his addiction had created.

Months prior to his entering the program, I had bought a 365-day prayer journal. Each day provided a scripture verse and lines for journaling. I'd never been one to journal, but I thought I'd give it a try.

When I turned to September 8 in the journal, I cried. The verse for that day, Galatians 5:1, became my anchor throughout his six months at the shelter. I knew God wanted Josh free of his chains, but I also knew I could do nothing to free him.

Although I realized I had no power to change my son, I still tried. I cried and bargained with God. I manipulated situations so he wouldn't face the consequences of his addictive choices: giving him money, paying his bills, making excuses for his behavior. I beat a dead horse time and time again, expecting a different outcome. I was trying to fix something that wasn't mine to fix.

Today's verse reminds us that Christ wants us free from

our chains of bondage. He desires that we stand strong against anything—drugs, alcohol, risky behaviors—that seeks to burden and rob us of opportunities to live victoriously. The verse says to "stand firm." How do we do that? As the family members, we stick to our standards of acceptable behaviors. We get counseling, if needed. A support group holds us accountable for maintaining our boundaries. We encourage one another to live one day at a time.

Our addicts stand firm by regularly attending Twelve Step meetings, getting a sponsor, and whatever else it takes to remain clean and sober. Your loved one may need to change locations and move out of state if necessary. A job change may be required because the current work environment is unsafe. Sobriety is not easy or comfortable. If it were, the AA and NA rooms would be empty. The addict's commitment to clean and sober living must be top priority.

Freedom is attainable and sustainable—one day at a time.

DAILY PRAYER

Dear Father, thank you for sending your Son to free us from bondage. Give me courage daily to walk in your freedom. Help me extend grace to my addict as he discovers the freedom you offer. Amen.

REFLECTION

Write your definition of freedom. Describe the harness your family is in.

DAY 72: JOY IN THE MORNING

"Weeping may remain for a night, but rejoicing comes in the morning."

Psalm 30:5b NIV

I cried myself to sleep more than one night over my son's behavior. As a matter of fact, I've wept many tears for all three of my children. Their choices baffled me, and I felt helpless to correct what was happening. Memories of lying in bed, weeping and calling out to God for help, with tears pooling in my ears, are still recallable.

Darkness covers the glorious light of the sun, creating shadows and illusions of reality. The night welcomes our tears and feeds hopelessness. We burrow under the covers like a frightened puppy and refuse to face the reality of our loved one's addiction. The darkness is our friend.

Then the sun comes up, shedding its brilliant rays, dispelling night's gloom. Shadowy figures creating fear in the dark vanish in the glare of morning. Our perspective changes as night melts away.

A new day allows us to gather our thoughts as we consider the most recent incident with our addict. Once we've released our initial emotions through tears or other ventings, we can rationally figure out what steps to take. There is wisdom in saying, "I think I'll sleep on it." After any particularly stressful event, consider delaying heavy decisions until you've had a chance to thoughtfully weigh available options, looking at all angles. Letting some time elapse provides a more reasoned perspective.

I share a few quotes about darkness and light with you as a source of inspiration:

"Beautiful light is born of darkness, so the faith that springs from conflict is often the strongest and the best" (R. Turnbull).

"Dare to reach out your hand into the darkness, to pull another hand into the light" (Norman B. Rice).

"I will love the light for it shows me the way. Yet I will endure the darkness for it shows me the stars" (Og Mandino).

The quote by Og Mandino says to me that walking in the light is preferred, but beauty is found even in the dark. As we live with an addict in our midst, it's certainly easier when we are in the light of recovery—with no drugs, no alcohol, and no risky behavior. But, we can also find strength in the dark times. It is during those trials we realize how strong our faith is and how courageous we are.

The dark times are tolerable knowing "joy comes in the morning."

DAILY PRAYER

Father of Lights, thank you for your promise of joy with the sunrise. Nights of crying are long and lonely, but I will endure because you are with me. Amen.

REFLECTION

Recall a recent night of weeping over your addict. How did you view the situation when the sun came up?

DAY 73: HEAVENLY REMINDERS

The Pillar of Cloud by day and the Pillar of Fire by night never left the people.

Exodus 13:22 MSG

Ping. The sound signaled an incoming text message. I looked at my cell phone screen and saw that Josh had sent me a picture of a beautiful cloud formation. When I saw the cloud, I started crying. My memory whisked me back to a day when he was seventeen or eighteen years old.

My husband and I were driving Josh home from a facility in another county where he had spent ten days detoxing from drugs and alcohol. "Mom, look at the clouds. I can't believe how big and white they are. I've never really noticed them before. Maybe now that my head's clear I'll notice things like that."

Clouds. Something as simple as a cloud had caught his attention once his mind's eye wasn't operating in a haze of drugs. Fifteen years later, he still looks to the clouds for inspiration, reveling in a long-sought clarity of mind, soul, and body. He also remembers my love of clouds.

One morning in 2009 as I drove to work, I was praying and crying for Josh. His addiction was in full tilt mode, and I was calling out to God for help. I noticed a contrail in the shape of a cross, white against the bright blue sky. I managed to take a picture of it on my cell phone and sent it to Josh. Again God spoke to us through a cloud. The cross in the sky confirmed God was in control of the situation. I was reminded the power that raised Jesus from the dead was the same power available to deliver my son from the clutches of his addiction. I took great consolation from the clouds that day.

As the children of Israel fled through the desert to escape Pharaoh, God promised to guide them. He appeared as a pillar of cloud by day and a pillar of fire at night. By following the cloud's leading, the Israelites were led out of Egypt to safety. After God miraculously led them through the Red Sea on dry ground, they restored their trust in Him.

He still leads his children to safety today. He longs to point us in the right direction. Will we allow him to guide us?

Every time I look at clouds, I'm amazed at their beauty and recall God's goodness to my family. The clouds' continual motion whispers to my heart that God is always moving on our behalf. Just as the clouds aren't glued to the sky, neither is God's movement in my life stagnant.

Do you have a special reminder of God's presence? Remember a time when you felt His spirit moving in your life. Allow it to be a spiritual landmark of his love and care for you.

DAILY PRAYER

Father, thank you for guiding me each day. I thank you for the beauty of the clouds and for the reminder of your presence. Guide my loved one today as he seeks your face. Amen.

REFLECTION

Try cloud watching as a relaxation exercise. See if you can identify animals and other objects in the formations.

DAY 74: SAFE PARTNERSHIPS

By yourself you're unprotected. With a friend you can face the worst. Can you round up a third? A three-stranded rope isn't easily snapped.

Ecclesiastes 4:12 MSG

I stumbled upon a website called "Moms of Addicts" and registered my email address. It is a sisterhood of broken hearts for moms whose children are addicted and who feel lost and alone in their struggles. My heart ached as I read entry after entry, feeling each mother's brokenness. Spread across America, we mothers are connected by a common thread—love for our addicted children—and our frustration and heartache over them. We are a multi-stranded cord of mothers available to support one another, even though it is a virtual cord.

The website makes it possible to private message one another and offer more personal words. The discussion forums allow us to offer solace to a mom with a particular burden or situation to face: a child in jail, a child coming out of treatment, a child running away, and a child losing his or her battle through death. The problems are as varied as the families represented. We peck out our concern one computer key at a time.

Better still are face-to-face relationships with parents or spouses of addicts. We can offer words of encouragement from our own strength, hope, and experience. We understand each other, and that gives us courage to face difficult days. We pat a shoulder, hug a neck, or hold a hand.

The three-cord philosophy is evident in Twelve Step groups as the "you are never alone" message. The writings in the *Big Book* and *Basic Text* encourage fellowship among the alcoholics and addicts. Bill W., one of the founders of Alcoholics Anonymous, recognized early on the strength in numbers. As he reached out to other alcoholics, his own recovery was strengthened and sustained.

If you are not part of a support group or Twelve Step group and struggle with aloneness, I'd encourage you to find one in your community. Don't be discouraged if there isn't one in your area. Contact whichever organization you need online and express your desire to start a group. You'll receive a beginner's packet to learn how to gather your support base.

Become a part of a three-cord strand offering strength to a fellow parent or spouse whose heart is broken because of addiction. You'll be stronger for it.

DAILY PRAYER

Dear Lord, I want to be a part of something strong and helpful, part of a solution. I want to be part of a three-cord strand that will offer strength and protection. Guide my loved one to find someone with whom he can form a safe partnership. Amen.

REFLECTION

Think about the people who form your three-stranded rope. Write down what makes them special. Let them know how much their support means to you.

DAY 75: LOOKING FOR THE GOOD

You intended to harm me, but God intended it for good to accomplish what is now being done, the saving of many lives.
Genesis 50:20 NIV

The Old Testament story of Joseph and his older brothers applies to us today. His brothers were jealous of the special attention he received from their father, and they plotted to kill him. Some of the brothers got cold feet about murdering Joseph, so they threw him into a dried up well, smeared his prized coat of many colors with animal blood, and told their father a wild animal had killed him.

Actually, they sold him into slavery to rid themselves of their father's favorite son. However, God worked in Joseph's life to elevate him to a place of great responsibility in Egypt. Through a series of events, Joseph and his brothers were reunited. After their father's death, the brothers feared Joseph's retaliation.

But he assured them God had translated the harm they originally intended for him into victory. He had become second in command in Egypt and provided food to them during the famine.

How many of us can say that about life with our addict? Can we stop and remember the past in the light of our present? We often get caught up in the yuck and pain of addiction and miss the blessings hidden between the tears.

My family's experience with rebellious teenagers and an addict son, while not what I wanted, has not been without reward. My view of people changed as a result of the last several years. I realize now that just because someone is smiling on the outside, the person's heart can be breaking. I've become a better listener, careful to discern the real emotions in someone's story. I've confidently comforted discouraged mothers out of the hope I have in God's promises of restoration.

When you discover nuggets of hope, share them with someone else, even through your own despair. Let them know that what the enemy meant for harm—to destroy their family—God turned around to bring Him glory. Share with those around you how your family survived the onslaught of addiction. Your story may be the nudge another family needs to dig in their heels and do battle.

DAILY PRAYER

Dear Father of turnabouts, thank you for your faithfulness to make something beautiful out of a messy life. Amen.

REFLECTION

Jot down ways in which the struggles and challenges you've experienced with your addict have been turned around for good purposes.

DAY 76: MORSELS OF GRACE

Taste and see that the Lord is good; blessed is the man who takes refuge in him.

Psalm 34:8 NIV

When I was eight or nine years old, I visited my Aunt Patsy and Uncle Roland for a week. We went to the grocery store to get some apples for my uncle. To an eight year old, an apple is an apple. I didn't know there were different varieties of the fruit.

"We need to get Red Delicious apples," Aunt Patsy said. She picked up several red apples, inspecting each one before placing it in the plastic bag.

"How do you know it's delicious if you haven't tasted it?" I asked her. My aunt got a good laugh from my question, along with the rest of the family as it was retold.

Recovery is much like my innocent question about apples. How do you know how good or rewarding clean and sober living can be unless you've tried it? Our addicts can listen to testimonies and stories told by addicts about how their lives were changed by practicing the Twelve Steps or going into a treatment program. But until they experience life change through their own recovery, they are just stories.

As family members, we can do everything we can to encourage our loved ones to give recovery a chance. Offering to attend a meeting may be the boost they need to take a positive step toward wholeness. Perhaps you can offer to babysit if they are using lack of childcare as an excuse not to attend Twelve Step meetings.

Think of as many practical ways as you can to assist your loved ones to get that first bite of sobriety. Could you take them to a meeting? Provide two or three names of addiction counselors and encourage your loved one to make an appointment with the counselor of choice. Offer to pet sit if that allows the addict a chance to go to a treatment program. I don't like cats, but I offered to cat sit while my friend was away four months in treatment. A few months of inconvenience on my part were worth her sobriety.

Think of recovery as broccoli. Many people say they don't like broccoli, but they've never tasted it. Once they try it, they like it and want more. The same philosophy applies to recovery. The thought of sobriety needs to be attractive and enticing enough to compel them to attend an initial meeting. Your addict needs to get a few days or weeks clean and sober under his or her belt. The recovery slogan, "Keep coming back. It works if you work it," ties in with today's verse.

Taste and see what God has in store for you and your addicted loved one. Encourage him or her to continue doing the next right thing, taking small bites each day of God's goodness and promises.

DAILY PRAYER

Dear Father, thank you for the morsels of grace you provide. They make me long for more and more. I pray my loved one samples your goodness and begins a steady diet of your Word. Amen.

REFLECTION

Write down a time when you experienced God's goodness. Describe how your faith was bolstered.

DAY 77: THE SWEET SMELL OF RECOVERY

I am a rose of Sharon, a lily of the valley.

Song of Solomon 2:1 NIV

Within the tightly wound petals of a rose lies a promise of great beauty. I have a rosebud friend, a full bloom in the making.

We met eleven years ago while collecting the mail from our respective home mailboxes. We exchanged safe greetings, "Hello, how are you doing?" The years wore away the surface comments and friendship grew. The more time we spent together, the more obvious her ever-increasing addiction problem.

I finally confronted her about the behaviors I observed from my side of the street. She agreed she needed help. I made a call to a treatment center to check on bed availability. "Tell her to come on Tuesday." She checked in, and life change began. The rose was planted.

Four months later, I sat in the audience as she graduated the program. Amid laughter and tears, she said goodbye to women who experienced similar problems and with whom she shared the promise of a brighter future. The time had arrived to go home and face the real world.

Two days out of treatment, her dishwasher hose broke, flooding the kitchen, adjoining dining and living rooms, and her recently laid hardwood floors. Normally an event such as this would be an excuse to get high, but she handled the crisis like a champ.

I've watched her recovery blossom since coming home. She attends NA and AA meetings, has a sponsor, studies her Bible every day and is volunteering at a church. The rosebud is slowly unfurling and its beauty is a marvel to behold.

Today's verse has many explanations. One fitting for recovery concerns the Plain of Sharon in Israel where this rose grows. It is not a rich soil, but rubbish. The roses from this area are noted for their great fragrance and abundance of blooms. Many times addicts live their lives in what the world considers rubbish and are treated as trash, but when they experience recovery they emit a fragrance that is far-reaching and attractive. Their perfume touches others as they live out their recovery, one day at a time.

Do you have a rosebud in your life on the verge of bursting forth, or do you have a handful of thorns? It's worth the pain of working around the thorny issues that arise when dealing with an addict. When they finally "get it," when the light bulb turns on in their heads, the rewards for persevering are worth every thorn prick you experience.

DAILY PRAYER

Dear Lord, thank you for loving me in spite of the thorns in my life. Help me to love my addict with the same kind of love and grace. Thank you for the beautiful fragrance of recovery and its ability to reach others with its promise of new beginnings. Amen.

REFLECTION

Write down some names for Jesus, starting with Rose of Sharon. Think about how the names reflect his character. Consider how the different attributes of Christ can help you through a difficult period.

DAY 78: STANDING ON PRINCIPLE

Don't become so well adjusted to your culture that you fit into it without even thinking.

Romans 12:2a MSG

Most people want to fit in and be accepted, especially by the popular crowd. When does the desire or pressure to fit in occur? It seems the age drops lower every year.

A young woman recently called me about a dilemma she and her husband had with their ten-year-old son. He wanted to purchase an updated version of a particular video game. Several of the boy's friends had it. A sleepover was planned, and the boys would play the game on their handheld devices. Her son wasn't invited because he's not allowed to play the video. He was excluded.

She cried as she said, "I want him to be popular and have friends, but I don't want him viewing the violence and hearing the profanity on the video. What do we do?"

"What do we do?" Parents have asked that question for years, longing for a good answer. We want our children to be accepted by their peers but at what price?

As our children were growing up, I know that I caved to their pleadings to have what their friends had or to go where their friends were going for the same reasons as my friend lamented: I wanted them to be part of the crowd.

My son Josh and I discussed my friend's situation, and he said, "I think she should stick to her guns. He'll have friends, probably more than he'll know what to do with. Look at me; I had too many friends and look where it got me."

Josh's need for acceptance and approval drove many of his poor choices throughout his teens. He sacrificed his principles and his upbringing for the label of being popular. My son was no different from those I tagged as the "bad kids."

Parenting is tough work and it's not getting any easier. Temptations are now a mouse click away, making it imperative for families to set and monitor boundaries.

In today's verse, Paul cautions the Romans not to be arrogant in their non-conformity. We sometimes become prideful because we don't participate in what some say are "sinful" behaviors. Pride is not an admirable quality, and Paul warns that we should check our motives for our decisions.

Discuss your values with your children and how they've shaped your family's values. Listen to their responses and work together to meet their needs for peer acceptance while maintaining your principles.

DAILY PRAYER

Dear Father, it is difficult to be a non-conformist. Give me wisdom and courage to guide my family in ways that are pleasing to you. Bless my addict as he makes tough decisions to stand on godly principles instead of being one of the crowd. Amen.

REFLECTION

In what ways do you conform to the culture around you? Have you compromised your principles to fit in with the crowd? How about your addict's conformity?

DAY 79: LOSING THE WORRY LIST

Give your entire attention to what God is doing right now, and don't get worked up about what may or may not happen tomorrow. God will help you deal with whatever hard things come up when the times comes.

Matthew 6:34 MSG

I used to almost brag about being a worrier. "I worry about everything, all the time," I'd say. After reading Jeremiah 30 and 31 back in 2009, it finally dawned on me that God was a purveyor of peace and not worry. My fretting days ended then.

That's not to say I don't play the *what if game* on occasion, but my mind is not consumed by negative, nagging thoughts day in and day out.

There was a time in my life when I was almost paralyzed by worry over my children. When they were late getting home, I knew they were dead. I rehearsed the phone calls I would make to our parents, telling them one of the kids was dead. I'd envision their funerals and how I would handle it. I worried myself almost sick.

The things I imagined didn't come to pass. But, in the process of worrying, I was robbed of peace, joy, and happiness. I also contributed to the strife in our home because of my constant yammering about what the kids were doing and where they were going.

We've already discussed the Twelve Step philosophy of living one day at a time, but it bears repeating. Bill W. was wise in formulating that guiding principle to live one day at a time. We can live only within a given moment; projecting into the future what might happen is futile. In fact, it's scriptural to let tomorrow take care of itself (Matthew 6:34).

Another familiar scripture about worry is found in Matthew 6:25-27. This passage is part of the Sermon on the Mount in which Jesus reminds the people that worrying about food and clothes is useless. He takes care of the birds, insignificant creatures, so why wouldn't he take care of humans, his prized creation? Jesus asks the question, "Does worrying add an hour to your life?" Of course, the answer is "No." If anything, constant worrying robs us of our lives. Headaches, stomach problems, and high blood pressure often have their roots in an overactive worrisome imagination.

As you live each day in the shadow of your loved one's addiction, remember these scriptures and be encouraged. Concentrate on the areas that you can affect—your responses to situations and maintaining proper boundaries.

Can you identify things or situations you worry about? Write down your worry points and then pray specifically that God will help you lay them down. Use today's scriptures as your prayer. Thank God that he clothes and feeds you. Because of His faithfulness in that area, you know he will be faithful to take care of you and your addicted loved one.

DAILY PRAYER

Dear Lord, thank you for your daily provision. I thank you that you care as much about meeting my needs as you do the birds flying in the air. As I read your Word, help me believe that you will relieve my worrisome nature. Thank you for your faithfulness and promises. Amen.

REFLECTION

List the things you worry about most. How many of them have happened?

DAY 80: A REAL THANKSGIVING

"We have here only five loaves of bread and two fish," they said. Jesus said, "Bring them here to me."
Matthew 14:17-18 NIV

An apron-clad server escorted our family to a round, gray table adorned with scalloped-edged paper placemats. Cheap institutional silverware lay atop white paper napkins like tin soldiers at attention. The small silk flower arrangement looked lonely. The cold chair sent shivers through my pants legs when I sat down.

Welcome to Thanksgiving Dinner 2000 in a treatment center.

Our server set prepared plates on the placemats; we didn't choose our food. The plate contained turkey, dressing, green beans, and mashed potatoes. I don't remember the dessert, but it was probably store-bought pumpkin pie.

I was humiliated sitting at that plastic table on a plastic chair having my meal served by a stranger. How did I end up in a place that stood in stark contrast to Thanksgiving dinners past?

My son was in a homeless shelter that provided an addiction recovery unit for men. Having lunch at the shelter was the only way to share Thanksgiving dinner as a family. My thoughts raced as I looked around at families vastly different from mine, yet much the same.

In spite of the humiliation, my heart overflowed with thankfulness for the men and women who ministered to us that day. The occasion rang with promise of new beginnings for our son and our family. I didn't want to be there, but I was grateful a place existed for people in need.

I recall my "aha moment" that Thanksgiving Day. I realized that addiction could happen to anyone, not just the poor and homeless. Who would have thought our middle-class family would one day gather around a table in a homeless shelter to celebrate Thanksgiving?

I'm thankful for that day because it changed me. It chipped away at my pride. Before this experience, I didn't hold a high opinion of addicts. My thoughts are different now. I've witnessed firsthand my son's struggles and know how difficult living sober—one day at a time—can be.

Thanksgiving 2012 found our family gathered around a mahogany dining room table blanketed with a colorful cloth. A handcrafted arrangement of fresh flowers and fall leaves added to the festiveness. We chose the food for our plates, and I remember well Mother's decadent desserts.

I whispered a prayer for families separated at Thanksgiving, Christmas, and other holidays or those who find themselves sitting around a plastic table served by volunteers. I am grateful for the blessings of the day.

DAILY PRAYER

Dear Father, thank you for family times around the dinner table. Thank you for blessing us with memories of good food and fellowship. I pray that my loved one will find himself in a safe place when separated from the family. Thank you for those who meet his needs and bless them for their service to the down and out. Amen.

REFLECTION

Describe a meal you shared with people whom you didn't know. How did you feel about the arrangement?

DAY 81: LOOKING FOR THE LOST ONE

What do you think? If a man owns a hundred sheep, and one of them wanders away, will he not leave the ninety-nine on the hills and go to look for the one that wandered off?

Matthew 18:12 NIV

My mother's intuition kicked into overdrive one afternoon when I got home from work and Josh wasn't there. He had begun hanging out at a local theater with some guys I didn't know and the association made me uneasy. I assumed he was with them, and up to no good, so I decided to go looking for him.

Sure enough, I pulled up by the curb in front of the theatre and there he was—with *them.* They were sitting on a ledge smoking cigarettes, laughing, and talking. When he saw me drive up, he almost swallowed his cigarette. Busted.

I am a non-confrontational person and never want to cause a scene in public or otherwise embarrass myself or my children. After all, Southern belles don't misbehave in public! I couldn't help myself that day. I went stomping up to him, not really caring if he was embarrassed, and demanded he get in the car. My index finger looked like a metronome on high speed wagging in his face. "You get yourself in that car, and I mean right now!"

He complied. The ride home was quiet because I knew better than to talk as angry as I was. We later discussed the incident. He apologized and said he understood my concerns.

Today's verse popped into my head that day. As I was out looking for my son, I remembered the story of the shepherd looking for the one lost sheep. He had ninety-nine others back in the pen, so what was so important about one missing sheep? Just that, the sheep was lost, and the shepherd wanted him back with the flock.

When we have a lost child or spouse in our midst, the temptation is sometimes to let them go their own way. We've chased after them time and time again, and they remained in the wilderness. We may have other children doing the right things, so why not concentrate on them and let the errant one wander away? Because that lost sheep is the one who needs help in finding his or her way back home. Jesus didn't give up on me, and I didn't give up on my son.

"The squeaky wheel gets the oil" applies to families dealing with an addict. The family member with the problem gets most of the attention. If not careful, resentment within the family festers and creates a whole other set of issues demanding attention. We have to find balance within our family system so those who are not lost are not overlooked.

Lost sheep need a shepherd. Gently guide your loved one back, remembering to strike a balance with other family members.

DAILY PRAYER

My heavenly Shepherd, thank you for looking for me when I was lost. Thank you for watching over my lost sheep as he wandered in the wilderness. Thank you for bringing him home. Amen.

REFLECTION

Recall a time when you lost something valuable. What steps did you take to search for it?

DAY 82: ONE MORE LOOP AROUND

... Let us run with perseverance the race marked out for us.

Hebrews 12:1b NIV

A picture of my son was posted on Facebook in October 2012, almost three years to the day when I read Jeremiah 30 and 31. The irony of the two didn't dawn on me until this moment while typing these words. The picture showed him with co-workers completing a triathlon. That's right, a triathlon.

Our family's restoration process has taken some strange turns over the last three years, but I never envisioned my son running a race. Field and track never interested him as a kid. One of his aversions to sports included his dislike of running. Since the triathlon, he has run in a 5K-benefit race and plans to continue running.

Today's verse includes a word at the very heart of recovery: *perseverance*. Dictionary.com defines the word as "steady persistence in a course of action, a purpose, a state of mind, and so forth, especially in spite of difficulties, obstacles, or discouragement." That sounds like the elements of recovery.

The sport of running demands persistence. A runner builds speed and endurance by hitting the track day after day. The runner knows that each foot planted in front of the other takes him closer to the finish line.

Our loved ones are running the race of their lives, for their lives. These special people, whom we love, build months and years of sobriety by hitting the recovery track twenty-four hours a day, every day. They know regardless of the environment, safe or unsafe, the track before them is what matters.

As family members, we also run an endurance race. The track may take the shape of a courtroom. We persist in love by supporting with our presence, not necessarily our resources. We may make a loop around a hospital emergency room when our loved one overdoses, but we stand beside the hospital bed, praying for survival. We persist in spite of the difficulties we face. We keep our eyes on the prize: recovery and restoration.

Steady persistence is not for the faint-hearted. Grab your water bottle and prepare for the run of your life.

DAILY PRAYER

Dear Father, thank you for filling me with staying power with my loved one. When times of discouragement overwhelmed me, you nudged my spirit to take another step, to make another loop around the track called recovery. Fill my loved one's heart with the desire to persevere in recovery. Make him a solid winner. Amen.

REFLECTION

Training for a race requires hard work and preparation. How have you prepared yourself for living with an addict?

DAY 83: THE ROOTS OF BITTERNESS

See to it that no one misses the grace of God and that no bitter root grows up to cause trouble and defile many.

Hebrews 12:15 NIV

Kudzu is a nuisance vine common in the South. It was introduced to the United States in 1876 by Japan in celebration of America's 100th birthday. What started as a gesture of goodwill turned into an environmental nightmare. Some say it's the vine that ate the South.

The vines are aggressive in growth and reach. If left untended, they can completely encase a house. Perhaps you've seen trees blanketed with the luscious green leaves while traveling southern roads. Telephone poles and the connecting cables look like giant green scarecrows as the kudzu creeps up and over them. The dense foliage prevents the sun's penetration to the trees and plants beneath the vine, and the vegetation dies.

For successful, long-term control of kudzu, the root crown and the rooting runners must be destroyed. The crown is a fibrous knob of tissue that sits on top of the root. Crowns form the vine nodes that root to the ground. According to Wikipedia.com the older the crown, the deeper the roots are in the ground because they are covered by sediment and plant debris.

Much like kudzu root crowns, bruised and buried emotions percolate with problems. Emotions are God-created and well-managed most of the time, but what happens when someone hurts our feelings or offends us?

We start harboring resentments. We begin to put down angry roots of envy or hatred. We keep a record of infractions against us. We allow the kudzu of bitterness to invade our hearts. Before long, just like trees and telephone poles, we're covered up in bitterness, and there's no end to the damage it will do.

Your addict has inflicted great hurt on you and your family. Protective calluses cover your heart to keep out another dart of disappointment and pain, but God wants to scour away the rough spots, leaving fertile ground for new relationships.

Ridding a field of kudzu vines is costly and time consuming. So it is with our hearts. There's only one way to get it done—take the first step. Pick up your emotional shears and start chopping away at the roots of bitterness. Allow the warmth of God's love to shine through and nourish you back to wholeness.

DAILY PRAYER

Dear Lord, point out the roots of bitterness in my heart today. I will turn them over to your pruning shears so that I can grow and encourage others instead of defiling them with my bitterness. Amen.

REFLECTION

Describe ways in which bitterness creeps into your life. What can you do to keep bitterness in check?

DAY 84: THE "SO THAT" STORY

Praise be to the God and Father of our Lord Jesus Christ, the Father of compassion and the God of all comfort, who comforts us in all our troubles, so that we can comfort those in any trouble with the comfort we ourselves have received from God.

2 Corinthians 1:3-4 NIV

Advertisers spend billions of dollars promoting creature comforts. We use fabric softeners to keep scratchy fabrics from irritating our skin. We spend thousands of dollars on luxury cars that promise a smooth ride. Movies can be viewed from the comfort of our homes, no more hassle of standing in line for a ticket and having your feet rest on a sticky theatre floor. Mattress companies promise a restful night's sleep. These are examples of reducing discomfort or pain.

Today's scripture doesn't promise the removal of discomfort. Some may think Paul meant God's comfort would erase all pain and suffering. But that's not the message. Paul tells the Corinthians that God will comfort them in all their troubles. Then why bother discussing comfort?

Look at verse 4 and the two words: so that.

So that is at the heart of Christianity and recovery. So that is the Twelfth Step of recovery. He comforts us so that we can comfort someone else in pain. The so that is why you are holding this devotional book in your hands. I want to share the comfort

God graciously poured into my life on October 8, 2009.

I cannot fix your child, husband, mother, or father. For that matter, I can't fix my child, but I can extend to others the hope and encouragement God offered to me. In the vernacular of recovery, I offer my "experience, strength, and hope." My experience tells me that my hope is in the promises of God's Word, and the joy of the Lord is my strength.

This season of your family's life has a purpose and place in God's timeline. You will be blessed as you share your experience, strength, and hope with other mothers, fathers, or spouses grappling with their loved one's addiction. Remember how you felt when someone at an Al-Anon or Nar-Anon meeting greeted you with a look of understanding? I imagine it's much like two battle-scarred veterans meeting in a parking lot. Soldiers don't need all the gory details to know they have a shared experience. Parents and spouses know the look of desperation all too well. They also need to recognize the look of hope.

Step Twelve says, "Having had a spiritual awakening as the result of the steps, we tried to carry this message to alcoholics, and to practice these principles in all our affairs."

Go and comfort with the comfort you have received. Share the message of hope.

DAILY PRAYER

Dear Father of all comfort, thank you for calming my bruised and battered heart. Thank you for opportunities to pay forward the grace and mercy you freely gave to me. In faith, I praise you for preparing a comforter for my loved one. Amen.

REFLECTION

Write down how you are comforted. Recall a time when you comforted someone in that way.

DAY 85: THREE LITTLE WORDS

And now these three remain: faith, hope and love. But the greatest of these is love.

1 Corinthians 13:13 NIV

1 Corinthians 13 is known as the Love Chapter in the Bible and often read at weddings and sometimes at funerals. We love to think, sing, and write about love. It makes our world go around. The apostle Paul verbalized for the world what love is and what love is not in this chapter. For families in recovery, a clear definition is crucial.

Love is patient. I quit praying for patience many, many years ago. Why? Because God would invariably answer the prayer by giving me a situation for which I needed patience. Love is patient, and it will be tested. Interruptions in our daily routines require patience. A child tugging on your pants leg while you're talking on the phone results in a raised voice, "Will you please wait just one minute? Don't you see I'm on the phone?" In retrospect, an interrupted phone conversation by a toddler is a minor irritation compared to the shenanigans of an out-of-control teenager.

Love is kind. Kindness grows out of patience. The child yanking at our pants leg needs to go to the bathroom, but his zipper is stuck. Patience with little fingers allows kindness to lean down and help without grumbling. Patience with our addict and understanding his or her desire to stop using allows kindness to look for a treatment center. Kindness implies empathy. We can rejoice with those who rejoice and weep with those who weep. Our hearts swell with compassion.

Paul also tells us what love is not: proud, selfish, rude, easily given to anger, or a record keeper of bad behaviors. These qualities are among the most difficult to overcome. We are prone to bouts of pride, selfishness, angry outbursts, and scorekeeping. I'm sure you've experienced all of these emotions and behaviors living with your addict. Keep in mind your addict has felt these coming from you too.

When we reach verse 13, Paul uses a word bridge, And now, to connect the preceding verses. It's almost as if he was saying, "Okay, we've talked about what love is and isn't. Now we're getting to the heavy stuff: faith, hope, and love."

Faith in God and love for our family keeps us getting out of bed each day. God is in control and has a plan. This knowledge gives us strength to do what needs to be done, to make wise decisions. Faith is the foundation on which we take a stand for the future.

Hope is born from our faith. Hope is reflected in our attitudes toward family members, friends, co-workers, and people in general. Based on our faith, we confidently look forward to tomorrow. As long as there is life, there is hope.

Love, the greatest of the three, is the action word. It's a choice we make every day. We can be patient or impatient, kind or unkind. We choose to love in spite of our addicts' behaviors.

They try our patience. They are selfish, angry, and critical of what we do or don't do. Loving them is our choice; they can't take that away. Isn't love grand?

DAILY PRAYER

Dear loving Father, thank you for loving me in spite of myself. I pray that I will love my addict out of a heart full of patience, faith, and hope. Give me your eyes to see him as you do. Amen.

REFLECTION

Explain why love is the greatest of the three attributes in today's scripture verse.

DAY 86: NEVER GIVE UP

And the Lord said, "I will wait until you return."
Judges 6:18b NIV

Several years ago, I was in a dark place spiritually and emotionally. From outward appearances, everything in my life was bright and rosy, but on the inside I was dead. I felt abandoned by God, if he even existed. I had reached a low place I had not visited for many, many years. I didn't know how much longer I could keep up the façade of "everything is okay."

Flipping through my Bible one day, I stumbled upon today's passage and cried when God spoke to me through His Word, "Sharron, I will wait until you return." The notation in my Bible says, "Thank you, Lord!" God gave me the room I needed to pull myself together through reading the scriptures and praying. He waited for me.

The context for today's verse illustrates where families of addicts find themselves. God told the Israelites to have nothing to do with the foreigners in the lands, but they disobeyed. For seven years foreign tribes dominated the Israelites and made their lives miserable.

We know what God's Word says about certain lifestyle choices, but we think we can beat the odds and do what everyone else is doing. That kind of thinking is a set up for problems.

We find Gideon hiding by a winepress when an angel appeared to him with startling news. God had chosen Gideon to save Israel from the Midianites. Gideon made excuses why he couldn't do the job. The angel's response was, "Go in the strength you have."

Do you ever hide from the realities of addiction? How can you charge the hill to victory when you're hiding from the reality of the situation? God wants us to walk in the strength we have. We might not get far, but at least we'll be moving toward a goal.

Again Gideon had an excuse for inaction, "My tribe is the smallest in Manasseh, and I'm the smallest in my family." The heavenly messenger said, "I will be with you."

We often think we can't effect change in our community because we are only one person or one family. Perhaps you can rally other families to join forces with you. When we stand before a city council, a judge, or family members, we can stand confidently knowing God is standing with us.

Gideon wanted a sign that he was really talking with the Lord, so he left to get a goat to sacrifice. He asked the messenger to wait for him to come back and the response was, "I will wait until you return."

Many of us are waiting for our loved ones to return. False starts toward recovery abound, and we grow weary. Disappointments stack up like firewood, higher and higher, as the waiting drags on. I waited many years for the day my son would come back to our family. It wasn't easy. The waiting didn't bring much joy, but it did bring results.

Assure your loved one you will wait for his return.

DAILY PRAYER

Dear Lord, thank you for waiting for me to make my way back to your loving arms. I pray for my loved one as he follows the path back home, one day at a time. Amen.

REFLECTION

How have you assured your loved one you will wait for them?

DAY 87: A SPIRITUAL DISCIPLINE

Yet when they were ill, I put on sackcloth and humbled myself with fasting.

Psalm 35:15 NIV

My husband and I had tried everything we knew to get our son clean and sober. We had put him in treatment centers, paid his bills, made excuses, cried, and prayed, but nothing we did made a difference. One thing we had not done was fasting.

Fasting was not a part of my religious upbringing. My current church had participated in a three-week Daniel Fast, and I survived the rigors of the discipline. I knew that the fast for Josh would be much different than a three-week Daniel Fast. It was about life and death.

On January 13, 2010, after reading Jeremiah 30 and 31 for the umpteenth time, I committed to fast all processed sugar until Josh was clean and sober for a year. I told God that if it took him ten years to get clean and stay clean for a year, then I was willing to go without sugar for ten years. I meant business; I wanted my son back.

I didn't tell anyone of my commitment. For four weeks I continued reading the two Jeremiah chapters and refraining from processed sugar. On February 18, 2010, Josh reentered the treatment center that had discharged him the previous November. He has been clean and sober since that day.

My venture into a sugar fast proved interesting on many levels. I soon realized how many foods, drinks, and snacks contain processed sugar. I also became aware of the strong temptations to eat those sugar-laden foods. I related these realizations to what my son, and addicts like him, face every day.

After a while, people began to ask why I didn't eat cakes and other sweets. I told them what I was doing and why. Opportunities to talk about addiction and recovery opened up, and I encouraged people to consider sobriety from a different perspective. If I had trouble staying away from sugar, something I loved, then imagine the pull of drugs and alcohol for our addicts. I have a new appreciation for those in successful recovery. It is truly a day-by-day decision to make right choices.

Drugs and alcohol are everywhere: school, church, work, and football games. Our addicts face daily, sometimes hour-by-hour choices to yield to the temptations surrounding them.

One of the happiest days of my life occurred on February 18, 2011, when Josh and I ate chocolate cake together in celebration of his one year of sobriety.

Would you prayerfully consider a time of fasting for your loved one?

DAILY PRAYER

Dear Lord, thank you for the experience of fasting. Thank you for using the experience to build my faith. I pray that others will find strength and solace in your promises and discover them to be true. Amen.

REFLECTION

Write down your thoughts regarding fasting. Consider if fasting is an appropriate spiritual exercise for you during this time of trial with your addicted loved one.

DAY 88: TREASURES OF THE HEART

But Mary treasured up all these things and pondered them in her heart.

Luke 2:19 NIV

I remember in vivid detail the day each of my three children was born. If I shut my eyes, I'm transported back in time to the morning Danny and I drove to the hospital to deliver our first child. I was scared beyond words. My parents joined us at the hospital to await the arrival of their first grandchild. I can almost feel the soft pressure of my newborn baby when she was laid in my arms. *I can't believe we have a baby. This little girl is ours. I'm a mother.*

The scripture tell us Mary, Jesus' mother, also recalled the events surrounding her child's birth. While her child was like no other, we mothers share the act of tucking away memories of our children's births and life events.

The verse implies she remembered the details of Jesus' birth, the treasures of that special night. I imagine as Mary witnessed the brutal beating Jesus endured at the hands of the Roman soldiers, flashes of his childhood crossed her mind. She watched in horror as the precious hands she had held as a child were pierced with spikes. The hair she had washed and combed hung wet and matted with blood. I imagine her mind remembered the day when Simeon blessed Jesus at his consecration in the temple. He told Mary, "And a sword will pierce your own soul too" (vs. 33). She contemplated those moments in time and recalled the old man's words as she beheld Jesus' crucifixion. I cannot fathom the pain Mary must have endured as Simeon's words came true on Golgotha's hill.

While our children's lives cannot compare to Jesus' life, like Mary, we recall moments of the innocence of our children and our dreams for their future. When Josh hit various low points in his addiction, this scripture would come to mind as I recalled his birth and early years. I ruminated on the special ways he made me laugh and how he loved playing with his dog Happy. Recalling the uncomplicated days before the addiction kicked in helped me get through those horrible times.

Ponder those heart treasures when your loved one is at his or her worst. Allow the sweetness of the memory to carry you through rough storms. Let your addict know about your moments of remembering the good times. Memories can create a longing for a return to a time before addiction.

DAILY PRAYER

Dear Lord, keeper of thoughts and memories, bless my ponderings tonight. I pray the times I remember are pleasing to you. As my loved one remembers life events, I pray pleasant memories will occupy more mental space than sad ones. In faith, I ask that you give us good memories in the days ahead. Amen.

REFLECTION

Recall a day you remember with extra special fondness—the day of your child's birth, graduation, or your wedding. Do you periodically replay the event in your mind?

DAY 89: THE GIVING OF HONOR

Children, obey your parents in the Lord, for this is right. Honor your father and mother—which is the first commandment with a promise—that it may go well with you and that you may enjoy long life on the earth.

Ephesians 6:1-3 NIV

My parents quoted today's verse often around our house of four children, but I never understood the difference in the two directives: obey your parents and honor your parents. Do you know what distinguishes the two words?

The words are similar to punish and discipline—one carries a negative connotation and the other implies correction and improved behavior.

To obey means that directions and rules will be followed. No questions asked; no back talk allowed. "Just do it because I said so," is what obey meant at my house growing up. Sometimes I questioned the reasoning behind a particular instruction. Daddy's consistent response was, "Don't dispute my word." I vowed when I grew up and had my own children, I'd never utter those four horrid words. I've said the dreaded four words many times through the years and have said them to my grandchildren.

Honor implies respect for the parental role. I don't think it means parents never make mistakes; it simply acknowledges the part parents play in a child's development. This is a way to say thank you for bringing me into the world, and for feeding, clothing, and providing shelter. Honor recognizes the long, sleepless nights spent holding a sick baby. It doesn't mean I agree with everything my parents did and said, but I will respect them.

When extreme misbehaviors occur within a family unit, respect and honor often fly out the door along with a tossed chair or dinner plate. Respect deteriorates rapidly when angry, hurtful words spew from mouths like water from a fire hydrant.

In all our years of dealing with errant teenagers, we never suffered verbal abuse or physical violence. I'm appalled at my friends' stories of their teenagers speaking disrespectfully to them. I'd still be blowing bubbles from having my mouth scrubbed with soap had I been verbally disrespectful to my parents! Television shows, movies, and music endorse disrespect, so it's no wonder our homes are full of ill-mannered family members.

The challenge for us is to fill this chink in our family's armor before our families fall into total anarchy. How? Start with teaching basic manners and saying "please" and "thank you." The basis of civility is the Golden Rule—treating one another as we want to be treated. Being kind to one another may not lead your loved one to put down his or her drugs, but it will take you a step closer to restoring a broken relationship.

DAILY PRAYER

Dear Father, thank you for parents who teach respect and kindness. Help me to live my life with my loved one so that honor and respect are the natural outflow of our years together. Amen.

REFLECTION

How have you taught your child to honor and respect you as his or her parent?

DAY 90: RESTORATION AT LAST

I have no greater joy than to hear that my children are walking in truth.

3 John 4 NIV

I've been chomping at the bit to write today's thoughts. No, not because it's the last entry. I want to tell you about my precious children, grown up and on their own. I want to move you beyond the cruddy things that happened to let you know God is faithful to fulfill his promises.

You've read how they misbehaved as teenagers and young adults and the resulting chaos in our family. Today I rejoice with the apostle Paul when I proudly proclaim, "I have no greater joy than to hear that my children are walking in the truth."

My oldest daughter, Caron, is married and has two children, Caleb and Caitlyn (my only granddaughter). Caron is a woman after God's own heart and has a passion for teaching his Word. She wrote a full-length Bible study she uses at a drug treatment center for women. She thought it was a domestic violence shelter. Imagine her surprise to discover it was for drug and alcohol abuse. Our family's experiences, coupled with her love for the Lord, enable her to minister in a unique way.

My son, Josh, about whom you've heard much, is well into recovery. When I wrote this entry, he had celebrated three years of clean and sober time. He has what I call a "miracle job." It's a miracle someone with his background would have his responsibilities.

Better than the miracle job, his marriage is being restored, and he is the father he always dreamed of being. He takes his son Cayden fishing and ice-skating. They play with neighborhood kids in the afternoons and build tree swings. He attends weekly NA meetings, has a sponsor, and sponsors others. He's active with the recovery community in our area and is paying forward what he's learned through the Narcotics Anonymous program.

My youngest daughter, Katie, has two sons, Kody and Mason, and is a baseball mom extraordinaire. Her job as a legal assistant keeps her busy. She loves those boys with all her heart and is a great mom. Katie is kind, loving, and grace giving. She looks for the best in others because she knows how it feels to have the negatives pointed out. She fights for the underdog. She loves long and she loves deep.

My children didn't graduate from college, but they did graduate from the School of Hard Knocks. The hard knocks were mostly of their own making, but those circumstances helped shape them into the wonderful young adults they are today. I wouldn't trade their sweet spirits and loving hearts for all the college diplomas in the world.

I thank God often for my daughter-in-law Misi's Facebook post: "Restoration Promised. Jeremiah 30 and 31." The strength and encouragement I received from reading and praying those two chapters changed my life and the life of my family.

If you are unable to echo Paul's joy over your addicted loved one, I pray that day will come soon for you and your family. The trials of a family living with an addict are painful, expensive, and unwanted. But I have learned over the past eighteen years that "God can do anything, you know—far more than you could ever imagine or guess or request in your wildest dreams!" (Ephesians 3:20 MSG).

When you feel like giving up, remember these verses from Jeremiah 31:15-17, "A voice is heard in Ramah, mourning and great weeping, Rachel weeping for her children and refusing to be comforted, because her children are no more. This is what the Lord says: 'Restrain your voice from weeping and your eyes from tears, for your work will be rewarded,' declares the Lord. 'They will return from the land of the enemy. So there is hope for your future,' declares the Lord. 'Your children will return to their own land.'"

May God bless you, one day at a time, as you wait expectantly for your loved one's return from the land of exile.

DAILY PRAYER

My dear, precious Heavenly Father, thank you for the children you entrusted to my care. I thank you for their stumbles in life because they led me to your throne of grace. I pray for other hurting families and ask that your peace surround them tonight and that their hearts are encouraged from reading your Word. I pray they experience your promised restoration. Amen.

REFLECTION

Recall occasions when someone bragged to you about your addicted loved one. How did you feel as you listened to positive affirmations instead of negative condemnations?

AFTERWORD

He is like a tree planted by streams of water, which yields its fruit in season and whose leaf does not wither. Whatever he does prospers.

Psalm 1:3 NIV

MEET MY HUSBAND

You've read about my children but little about my husband. I want you to know something about him as we close our time together.

Danny and I met in July of 1969 when I was sixteen and he was seventeen. My family owned a cottage at a private lake, and Danny was visiting his sister, who lived near our place. A friend and I were at the lake's beach area when Danny and his friend walked over to where we were sitting. "The rest is history," as the saying goes.

We dated through the remainder of high school and became engaged my senior year. The one requirement my daddy imposed was for us to finish college. Two and a half months after college graduation, I became Mrs. Danny Cosby.

My white picket fence dreams of marrying a doctor or lawyer and being wealthy didn't come true. My man became an executive with a Fortune 500 company and traveled extensively. He received a promotion that required a move from Alabama to Tampa, Florida, away from family and friends.

Danny's regular absences from our home opened the door for much of the misbehavior of our children. We both accept responsibility for lax parenting during that time, but it doesn't change the outcome. In 1997, when Josh's behavior was out of control, Danny made a life-changing decision. He walked away from his corporate career. He gave up the company car, the executive bonuses, and a host of other perks.

His decision was bathed in prayer. He didn't have a job waiting for him when he turned in the car keys. He had only time staring him in the face. In 1998 he made another life-altering decision: to pursue a career in addiction counseling. Talk about a 180° turn—from corporate executive to addiction counselor! I can tell you there were no bonuses or perks with this choice.

Together we attended a year-long addiction counseling training program in preparation for the Certified Addiction Professional state certification exam.

He has counseled hundreds of men and women, young and old, over the last several years, keeping in mind the pain our family experienced. He extends grace and hope to hurting parents and spouses.

Psalm 1:3 describes a tree planted by streams of water, and to me it's a picture of my Danny. Danny is my tree. He is the one I run to for shade when life gets rough and too much to handle. He is a godly man who doesn't keep wicked counsel. He meditates every day on God's Word and spends time in prayer for our family and his clients. The fruit he yields is changed lives.

I am eternally thankful that Danny and I had each other to lean on when the waves of despair crashed over us. When I was strong, he was weak, and looked to me for support. When I was weak, he was my rock. He wiped my tears and held me close on more occasions that I can count.

My prayer for you is that you will have support and encouragement when life's stressors weigh you down. Someone you can go to for comfort in times of trouble. Someone to go to bat for your loved ones when no one else will. A tree beside your troubled waters.

A WORD FROM JOSH

My name is Josh, and I am an addict.

I remember looking down at a Coke-can-turned-marijuana-pipe with a little bit of pot in it thinking, *should I be doing this?* I was in eighth grade. As I took in a deep breath, I remember feeling like I was finally a part of something.

That was how it all started. The middle of the story is a blur. It's been eighteen years of hurting myself and causing pain and hurt to everything that crossed my path. From the ages of thirteen to thirty, I spent my life hooked on one drug or another. I would change groups of friends and schools, running from the wreckage I had caused. My ability to clean myself up for a few days and lie without batting an eye kept me on the move and sick and for many years.

I remember waking up strapped to a hospital bed from an overdose with my parents standing over me sobbing. You'd think this would be enough to make a sixteen-year-old boy stop destroying his life, but addiction already had its hooks in me.

There were many times in my life when I would look at myself in the mirror and wonder, *How did I get here? Who is this person staring back at me?* The only skill I had to cope with these feelings was to use more drugs.

I rocked along having run-ins with the law, and bouncing from rehabs to homeless shelters, and family members' houses. I got married to an amazing woman during a stretch of clean time. We had our son in August of 2008 shortly after I started using again. It got real bad real quick.

I eventually destroyed our family. I moved to Sarasota, Florida, and started the journey to recovery. I joined a fellowship of people like me. They took me in and taught me how to stay clean. I don't know what was different about this time, except I finally had hope.

Hope was the thing I was always missing. Hope is what carried me through the nights of lying in bed missing my wife and son. Hope is what told me, *just stay clean, things will get better.* Hope is what got me to the point of being able to write this three years later sitting in my house with my wife upstairs and my son tugging on my leg to play with him. My life today is one I used to dream of. Not riches or fancy cars but one of love.

I have parents who fought to the end for me, two sisters who never gave up on me, a family of in-laws that, despite the pain I caused their daughter, showed me grace. I have a wife who loves me with all her heart and was able to forgive and a son who has a daddy. If I died today I would be okay. I am finally living a life that is worthy of the man God intended for me to be.

This journey I am on is one of constant work and upkeep. Today I have surrounded myself with positive people. My Mama always told me, "Show me your friends and I will show you your future." I have remembered her words many times during the past three years. Through working the Twelve Steps and staying with the winners, I now have a great job and am truly a productive member of the community in which I live. It's hard not to give all the credit to the family that stuck by me and forgave me over and over, but truly without God in my life I think I would be dead or in prison.

I pray a lot, but I'm no prayer warrior. I have found that having a personal relationship with God is the key. The prayer that started this whole recovery thing was, "God make this stop or let me die." My prayers are much different today.

Today I pray for other lost addicts to find the hope of recovery. I pray that the families reading this book will continue to have hope that an addict—any addict—can stop using drugs and find a new way to live.

If there is one thing I can say to family members it is, never quit fighting. There is always hope. With hope, I—a once "hopeless dope addict"—am now a "dope-less hope addict."

RESOURCES

Information about addiction is critical to understand the motivations of your loved one and to provide coping skills you will need along the way. The following books will help you acquire the information you need to successfully navigate life with an addict. There are other equally instructive titles available; these are a few I read and learned from.

The Big Book, A.A. World Services, Inc., 4th Edition, 2001

Narcotics Anonymous, Narcotics Anonymous World Services, Inc., 2008

The Five Love Languages, Gary Chapman, Northfield Publishing, Chicago, 2004

Addict in the Family: Stories of Loss, Hope, and Recovery, Beverly Conyers, Hazelden, 2003

Everything Changes: Help for Families of Newly Recovering Addicts, Beverly Conyers, Hazelden, 2009

Get Your Loved One Sober: Alternatives to Nagging, Pleading, and Threatening, Robert J. Myers, Ph.D. and Brenda L. Wolfe, Ph.D., Hazelden, 2004

The Addictive Personality, Craig Nakken, Hazelden, 1998

Beautiful Boy, David Sheff, Houghton Mifflin Company, 2008

Clean, David Sheff, Houghton Mifflin Company, 2013

For speaking engagements or further information, you may reach Sharron at:

P. O. Box 2123
Riverview, FL 33569
813-445-8201

www.efamilyrecovery.com
www.erecoverychurch.com

CPSIA information can be obtained
at www.ICGtesting.com
Printed in the USA
BVHW062134170119
538092BV00007B/539/P

9 781624 800719